Ubuntu Server Essentials

Unleash the true potential of Ubuntu Server in your
production environment using this administration guide

Abdelmonam Kouka

[PACKT] open source✲

community experience distilled

PUBLISHING

BIRMINGHAM - MUMBAI

Ubuntu Server Essentials

First published: November 2015

Production reference: 1251115

Published by Packt Publishing Ltd.
Livery Place
35 Livery Street
Birmingham B3 2PB, UK.

ISBN 978-1-78528-546-2

www.packtpub.com

Credits

Author
Abdelmonam Kouka

Reviewers
Dan Bishop

James A. Langbridge

Acquisition Editor
Larissa Pinto

Content Development Editor
Rashmi Suvarna

Technical Editors
Tejaswita Karvir

Vishal Mewada

Copy Editor
Vedangi Narvekar

Project Coordinator
Judie Jose

Proofreader
Safis Editing

Indexer
Hemangini Bari

Graphics
Kirk D'Penha

Production Coordinator
Melwyn Dsa

Cover Work
Melwyn Dsa

About the Author

Abdelmonam Kouka is a Tunisian computer engineer. He received his engineering diploma in computer science in 2007 from National School of Computer Sciences (ENSI), one of the best engineering schools in Tunisia. He received a master's degree in information security from the same school (ENSI) in 2009 and a master's degree in free and open source software from ISI/UVT in 2011. He received a master's degree in innovation management (the DICAMP.eu project) in 2014.

He was not just a student. In fact, after getting his engineering degree in 2007, in parallel to his master's marathon, he started working as a software developer in HR Access and then as a Zimbra consultant in another company. After that, he started to develop with Alcatel-Lucent as a Java/JEE developer to finish with Alcatel-Lucent as an IP/MPLS Expert. He left Alcatel-Lucent in December 2012 to launch, in partnership with his friend Ayed Akrout, his own startup named TAC-TIC (for more information, visit `http://www.tac-tic.net/`) that provides ICT services such as software development, open source consulting, and IP/MPLS engineering and support. He is also an Alcatel-Lucent University trainer who delivers advanced courses on IP platforms, fixed networks, and broadband access technologies.

While studying for engineering and during all of his professional experience, he was an open source activist; he was a member/co-founder of the Ubuntu-tn community, Sabily community, and the APOS association. He has also been a member of Linux Arabic Community, Arabeyes, CULLT, DFSA, and a lot of other open source clubs, associations, and initiatives.

He is also the author of *Learning Zimbra Server Essentials*, Packt Publishing, 2013.

I would like to give thanks and express my gratitude to my family; without their involvement, this book quite possibly would not have happened. A lot of thanks to my wife, Sonia, for her passion and patience with my late-night writing sessions. Also, a lot of thanks to my mother, Chadlia, and my brother, Iskander, for their encouragement and support during this work.

I dedicate this book to my lovely daughter, Mariem, whose smile is my source of inspiration.

Finally, to caffeine, my companion through many long nights of writing.

About the Reviewers

Dan Bishop is a systems administrator living and working in York, UK. He has extensive experience managing Ubuntu servers in personal as well as professional contexts, ranging from home office to enterprise. Apart from providing consultancy services to independent clients, he has forged a career in some of the top universities in the UK. Currently, he works at the University of York, developing a range of services that run on Ubuntu servers. In his spare time, Dan loves to travel the world, and he regularly volunteers as a special constable with the police.

James A. Langbridge does not like talking about himself in the third person, but he will try anyway. James was born in Singapore, and he followed his parents to several countries before settling down in Nantes, France, where he lives with his partner and their two children.

James is an author and embedded systems consultant. He has worked for more than 15 years on industrial, military, mobile telephony, and aviation security systems. He works primarily on low-level development, creating bootloaders or optimizing routines in assembly and making the most of small processors. When not on contract, James trains engineers to work with embedded systems and Linux. He enjoys making new gizmos, much to the dismay of his partner.

James wrote his first computer program at the age of six, and he has never stopped tinkering ever since. He began by using Apple IIs, ZX80s, and ZX81s, moved on to BBC Micros and the Amiga, and finally had no other option but to use PCs. He has been using Linux almost exclusively since 1995 and has no intention of changing. He has been using Ubuntu since 2006 as well as other flavors.

www.PacktPub.com

Support files, eBooks, discount offers, and more

For support files and downloads related to your book, please visit www.PacktPub.com.

Did you know that Packt offers eBook versions of every book published, with PDF and ePub files available? You can upgrade to the eBook version at www.PacktPub.com and as a print book customer, you are entitled to a discount on the eBook copy. Get in touch with us at service@packtpub.com for more details.

At www.PacktPub.com, you can also read a collection of free technical articles, sign up for a range of free newsletters and receive exclusive discounts and offers on Packt books and eBooks.

https://www2.packtpub.com/books/subscription/packtlib

Do you need instant solutions to your IT questions? PacktLib is Packt's online digital book library. Here, you can search, access, and read Packt's entire library of books.

Why subscribe?

- Fully searchable across every book published by Packt
- Copy and paste, print, and bookmark content
- On demand and accessible via a web browser

Free access for Packt account holders

If you have an account with Packt at www.PacktPub.com, you can use this to access PacktLib today and view 9 entirely free books. Simply use your login credentials for immediate access.

Table of Contents

Preface   **v**

Chapter 1: The Ubuntu Server Installation   **1**

Preparation before the installation   **1**

The latest Ubuntu release   1

System requirements   2

Additional resources   3

The manual installation   **3**

A simple installation from a CD   4

Upgrading from an old release   11

The advanced installation   **12**

Using RAID   13

Using LVM   14

The automated installation   **16**

The PXE process   16

The PXE installation procedure   16

Additional resources   20

Summary   **20**

Chapter 2: Configuring and Administering Ubuntu Server   **21**

Administering using the command line   **21**

The package management for an Ubuntu Server   **25**

Package repositories   26

Package management utilities   **28**

The dpkg tool   29

The aptitude tool   31

The apt tools   32

Adding software collections using tasksel   35

The network configuration for an Ubuntu Server   **36**

The configuration files   37

The network utilities   38

Performing essential system administration tasks	**40**
Monitoring resources	40
Processes management	43
Scheduling the processes that need to be run	44
Summary	**46**
Chapter 3: Deploying Servers on Ubuntu	**47**
Deploying an OpenSSH server	**47**
Installing the OpenSSH server	48
Configuring the OpenSSH server	48
Setting up a DNS server	**49**
The BIND installation	50
Ubuntu's BIND conventions	51
Configuring BIND	51
Zone file configuration	51
DNS redundancy	53
DNS testing	54
Turning on a web server	**54**
The LAMP Installation	55
Ubuntu's LAMP Conventions	56
Apache management and testing	58
apache2ctl	59
Stopping Apache gracefully	59
Diagnostic apache2ctl commands	59
Deploying an e-mail server	**60**
The MTA server	61
Installing Postfix	61
Managing Postfix	63
The MDA server	64
Filters and security for an e-mail server	**65**
Other facilities	68
Setting up a database server	**69**
The MySQL server	69
The Postgre server	70
Setting up a DHCP server	**70**
Installing DHCP	71
Ubuntu DHCP Conventions	71
Configuring DHCP	71
Installing a file server	**72**
The FTP server	72
The Samba server	72
Summary	**73**

Chapter 4: Security with Ubuntu   75
The basic security settings   75
Managing users   75
User account administration   76
Password administration   77
Permission settings   78
Applying quota to user accounts   81
Configuring administration tasks with sudo   82
Configuring the AppArmor tool   83
Advanced security configuration   87
SSH security enhancement   87
Configuring firewalls   89
Backuping and restoring   92
The principles of backup   93
Drive imaging   93
Database backups   94
Backup tools   96
Summary   100

Chapter 5: Virtualization and Cloud Computing inside the Ubuntu Server   101
Virtualization   101
An introduction to virtualization   102
The benefits of virtualization   102
Different techniques of virtualization   102
Type 1 hypervisor   103
Type 2 hypervisor   103
An isolator   104
The different approaches towards virtualization   105
Paravirtualization   105
Full virtualization   105
KVM (Kernel-based Virtual Machine)   105
Prerequisites   106
Configuring the KVM networking   107
The KVM installation   109
Managing virtual machines   110
XenServer   111
Prerequisites   112
Installing XenServer   113
The networking concept in a XenServer environment   114
Managing virtual machines   115
An introduction to Docker   116
How Docker works   116
Installing Docker   117
Using Docker   117

Cloud computing for the Ubuntu Server	**119**
The ownCloud software	119
The technology used in ownCloud	119
The ownCloud server installation	120
CozyCloud	121
Installing CozyCloud on the Ubuntu Server	121
Using CozyCloud	122
OpenStack	122
OpenStack tools	123
The OpenStack setup	124
Installing OpenStack using DevStack	124
The manual installation	125
Summary	**128**
Chapter 6: Tips and Tricks for Ubuntu Server	**129**
General tips	**129**
Ubuntu Server CLI tips and tricks	129
How to prevent server daemons from starting during installation	131
How to move or copy a directory	131
System resource limits	132
Running a command over and over	132
Troubleshooting tips	**132**
Customizing log rotation on Ubuntu Server	132
The main system log files	133
Checking opened files	134
Getting information from /proc	134
Recovering the root password under Ubuntu Server	135
Useful tools and utilities	**136**
NetHogs, a network monitoring tool	136
vnStat, a network monitoring tool	137
Tailing multiple files using multitail	138
The program cockpit – a remote manager for Ubuntu servers	138
Webmin - the famous system administration tool	139
Using the uvtool program and extending the use of Cloud images	140
Summary	**140**
Index	**141**

Preface

Ubuntu Server Essentials is a practical, hands-on guide that provides you with a clear step-by-step process to install and manage an Ubuntu Server, which will help you take advantage of the real power that is behind Ubuntu without being an expert in it.

This fast-paced book is for administrators who wish to discover the essentials of the latest version of the Ubuntu Server. The purpose of this book is to guide the readers so that they can deploy and configure Ubuntu servers in their office environments. First of all, we will start by explaining how to install the Ubuntu Server. Then, we will move on to cover the most useful aspect of the command-line interface that comes with it. Meanwhile, we will have a look at how to administrate and configure an Ubuntu Server. This knowledge will be extended with the help of a chapter dedicated to this topic. After that, we will discuss how to deploy services on an Ubuntu Server and secure it. Before finishing, we will discover the virtualization and Cloud computing facilities provided by Ubuntu. Finally, we will explore some very useful tips related to an Ubuntu Server.

What this book covers

Chapter 1, The *Ubuntu Server Installation*, serves as an Ubuntu Server installation guide.

Chapter 2, *Configuring and Administering Ubuntu Server*, provides the necessary knowledge and tools that are required to manage an Ubuntu Server.

Chapter 3, *Deploying Servers on Ubuntu*, allows users to easily set up and deploy a set of frequently used services, such as e-mail, the Web, DNS, and so on.

Chapter 4, *Security with Ubuntu*, serves as a security guide for the Ubuntu Server.

Chapter 5, *Virtualization and Cloud Computing inside the Ubuntu Server*, provides the knowledge needed to work with virtualization and Cloud computing.

Chapter 6, Tips and Tricks for Ubuntu Server, contains some of the most useful tips and tricks that every Ubuntu administrator needs.

What you need for this book

To use this book, you need only basic knowledge Linux OS and a cup of coffee.

Who this book is for

This book is intended for system administrators who are familiar with the fundamentals of the Linux operating system and are looking for a fast-paced guide on Ubuntu. Those familiar with the older versions of Ubuntu will also find this book useful. Basic knowledge of Linux administration is assumed. By the end of this book, readers will have a good understanding of working with the latest version of Ubuntu and exploring the new features of Ubuntu Server administration.

Conventions

In this book, you will find a number of text styles that distinguish between different kinds of information. Here are some examples of these styles and an explanation of their meaning.

Code words in text, database table names, folder names, filenames, file extensions, pathnames, dummy URLs, user input, and Twitter handles are shown as follows: "We can include other contexts through the use of the `include` directive."

A block of code is set as follows:

```
zone "localhost" {
  type master;
  file "/etc/bind/db.local";
  allow-transfer { 192.168.1.2; };
  also-notify { 192.168.1.2; };
};
zone "127.in-addr.arpa" {
  type master;
  file "/etc/bind/db.127";
  allow-transfer { 192.168.1.2; };
  also-notify { 192.168.1.2; };
};
```

Any command-line input or output is written as follows:

```
sudo ln -s /etc/phppgadmin/apache.conf /etc/apache2/sites-available/
phppgadmin
sudo a2ensite phppgadmin
sudo apache2ctl graceful
```

New terms and **important words** are shown in bold. Words that you see on the screen, for example, in menus or dialog boxes, appear in the text like this: "Then, go to the **Settings** of the machine and select the **System** tab."

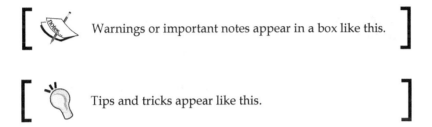

Warnings or important notes appear in a box like this.

Tips and tricks appear like this.

Reader feedback

Feedback from our readers is always welcome. Let us know what you think about this book—what you liked or disliked. Reader feedback is important for us as it helps us develop titles that you will really get the most out of.

To send us general feedback, simply e-mail feedback@packtpub.com, and mention the book's title in the subject of your message.

If there is a topic that you have expertise in and you are interested in either writing or contributing to a book, see our author guide at www.packtpub.com/authors.

Customer support

Now that you are the proud owner of a Packt book, we have a number of things to help you to get the most from your purchase.

Downloading the example code

You can download the example code files from your account at http://www.packtpub.com for all the Packt Publishing books you have purchased. If you purchased this book elsewhere, you can visit http://www.packtpub.com/support and register to have the files e-mailed directly to you.

Downloading the color images of this book

We also provide you with a PDF file that has color images of the screenshots/ diagrams used in this book. The color images will help you better understand the changes in the output. You can download this file from `http://www.packtpub.com/ sites/default/files/downloads/1234OT_ColorImages.pdf`.

Errata

Although we have taken every care to ensure the accuracy of our content, mistakes do happen. If you find a mistake in one of our books—maybe a mistake in the text or the code—we would be grateful if you could report this to us. By doing so, you can save other readers from frustration and help us improve subsequent versions of this book. If you find any errata, please report them by visiting `http://www.packtpub. com/submit-errata`, selecting your book, clicking on the **Errata Submission Form** link, and entering the details of your errata. Once your errata are verified, your submission will be accepted and the errata will be uploaded to our website or added to any list of existing errata under the Errata section of that title.

To view the previously submitted errata, go to `https://www.packtpub.com/books/ content/support` and enter the name of the book in the search field. The required information will appear under the **Errata** section.

Piracy

Piracy of copyrighted material on the Internet is an ongoing problem across all media. At Packt, we take the protection of our copyright and licenses very seriously. If you come across any illegal copies of our works in any form on the Internet, please provide us with the location address or website name immediately so that we can pursue a remedy.

Please contact us at `copyright@packtpub.com` with a link to the suspected pirated material.

We appreciate your help in protecting our authors and our ability to bring you valuable content.

Questions

If you have a problem with any aspect of this book, you can contact us at `questions@packtpub.com`, and we will do our best to address the problem.

1

The Ubuntu Server Installation

This chapter will cover how to install Ubuntu Server by using different methods. We will have a look at how to install Ubuntu Server in the manual and automated mode by using a simple or an advanced installation.

To reach this goal, we will follow this plan:

- Preparation before the installation
- The manual installation
- The automated installation

Preparation before the installation

In this section, we will take a quick look at the latest Ubuntu Server release news and then, we will make a list of all the system requirements.

The latest Ubuntu release

Canonical, the company that produces Ubuntu, releases a new version every 6 months. Each release has a code with a $YY.ZZ$ pattern, where YY is the year and ZZ is the month.

I started writing this book just after Ubuntu 15.04 (Vivid Vervet) was released on April 23, 2015. Currently, there are two major releases—the LTS one that was released last year (**LTS** stands for **long-term support**), which is version 14.04, and the latest version 15.04. It is not a big deal if you choose either of these two versions to perform the tasks in the coming chapters, since it will make no difference. So, we decided to use the latest version as a reference for our samples, especially because the next LTS release will be based on it. (Note that only the LTS releases are supported for 5 years by Canonical, and the non-LTS releases have a support of only 9 months. That's why we normally choose the LTS versions for Ubuntu Server deployments.) When there is a notable difference between these two versions, we will mention it.

Now, let's take a look at some information related to the latest version:

- It uses Linux kernel 3.19, which brings a lot of improvements in terms of performance as well as network facilities for both servers and cloud.

- 15.04 is the first Ubuntu version that features LXD.

- It uses the latest versions of OpenStack, **LXC** (**Linux Containers**), LXD, Juju, libvirt, QEMU, Open vSwitch, Ceph, cloud-init, Docker, and HA-related package updates.

- It replaced the service manager and the standard boot upstart with systemd.

> The upstart boot still exists under Ubuntu. You can use it by opening the **GRUB** boot menu, choosing **Advanced options for Ubuntu**, and then clicking on **Ubuntu, with Linux** (upstart).
>
> If you would like to switch permanently to the upstart boot, you can install the upstart-sysv package, which will remove ubuntu-standard and systemd-sysv.

System requirements

System requirements depend on the services that may need to be deployed in the future and installed on the server. For demonstration/test purposes, we need a minimal configuration of 300 MHz CPU, 192 MB of RAM, and a 1.5 GB hard disk. This light configuration allows us to deploy Ubuntu Server on an old computer or even a little virtual machine. This limited footprint is basically due to the absence of the X Windows System (graphic interface), which is not needed in a server environment.

In a production environment, you should be careful about your actual needs in terms of resources (the CPU, RAM, and hard disk) and the estimation growth of those needs. To do this, you need to make a good measure of dimensions based on the services that you are going to deploy.

In the case of the samples in this book, we will use the 64-bit version of Ubuntu Server 15.04, and we will install it on a virtual box machine that has 1 GB of RAM and 2 TB of hard disk.

 Note that if you are using a used computer/server, you should back up your data before installing or upgrading Ubuntu. Partitioning tools used in the installation process are reliable and can be used for many years without any problems in general, but sometimes, they can perform catastrophic actions.

Additional resources

This book comprises only the essentials. It contains exactly what you need to know to perform a specific task. If you need more information about and an in-depth understanding of Ubuntu, you can have a look at the official documentation by visiting `https://help.ubuntu.com`.

You should download the CD image according to your system architecture. The whole list exists at `http://releases.ubuntu.com/15.04/`.

The manual installation

In this section, we will have a look at how to install Ubuntu Server manually, either from the CD or the USB key. Here, we will only cover the installation from the CD; the same procedure applies for the installation from the USB key. In the latter case, you should configure your computer (using the BIOS interface) to boot from USB.

There is another way to manually install Ubuntu Server, which is via network, but since we will see this procedure in depth in the next **Automated installation** section, we will not cover it here.

A simple installation from a CD

The procedure for installing Ubuntu from a CD is the same as that for most of the Linux distributions. So, if you are familiar with this, you can save time and move directly to the next section. If you are a newbie in this field, please follow this section closely, since the next sections (advanced installation and automated installation) will be based on this. Note that for Ubuntu Server edition, there is no graphical environment like the one in the desktop edition. So, you will need to use only the keyboard and not the mouse. The stepwise procedure to install Ubunto from CD is as follows:

1. First of all, download the installation CD image that matches your CPU architecture from the download page at `http://releases.ubuntu.com/15.04/` and burn it on to an empty CD.

2. Secondly, verify that your server BIOS is configured to boot on a CD-ROM drive; if this isn't the case, take care that you change it.

3. Insert your CD in to the CD-ROM drive and boot it.

4. Just after the boot process starts, you will be asked to select the installation language. Choose the one that you want. Don't worry if you choose some other language by mistake. You will soon learn how to change the settings.

5. Now, you will get the following interface:

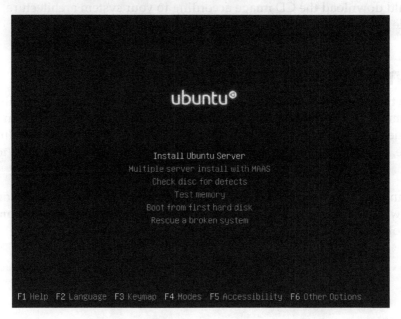

You can see a lot of options that cater to your needs:

- ° If you just press the *Enter* key when selecting the default **Install Ubuntu Server** option, you will start the installation process.

- ° The second option, **Multiple server install with MAAS**, will be covered later in the chapter when talking about virtualization and cloud.

- ° Some people prefer starting with the third option, **Check disk for defects**, to verify that the burn process of the ISO file on the CD was done correctly.

- ° The fourth option, **Test memory**, is very helpful, especially when your server starts crashing and you suspect a RAM-related problem.

- ° You can use the fifth option, **Boot from first hard disk**, to bypass the boot from the CD in case you forgot it by mistake in the CD-ROM driver.

- ° Finally, the last option, **Rescue a broken system**, turns a CD into a rescue disk that is useful for backup and recovery.

- ° In most of the cases, all that you need to do is launch the installation by pressing the **Enter** key when selecting the default **Install Ubuntu Server** option, but there are some cases where you need some special options, either because of some specific hardware-related need of your machine, or because you need to customize the kernel parameters of the server for future use. For this purpose, Ubuntu gives you a lot of possibilities via the bottom menu on the boot splash screen, which can be accessed via the function keys.

- ° If you press **F1**, you will see an interactive help screen with documentation for the rest of the options.

- ° If you accidentally chose the wrong language at the time of booting, press **F2** to change it. The boot screen will automatically choose a keyboard mapping based on your language.

- ° If you want a different mapping (for example, in my case, I am preparing screenshots for this book in English but I am using a French keyboard), press **F3** to choose from a list of keyboard mapping options. The boot screen also has a lot of great accessibility options.

- ° The **F4** key displays a list of installation modes from which you can choose to install Ubuntu Server by using an OEM installation, a minimal system, and a minimal virtualization guest. The OEM installation is available for manufacturers. The minimal virtualization guest gives you an easy way to install a virtualized version of Ubuntu.

°   The **F5** key shows an accessibility menu that allows you to choose a high-contrast screen, a screen magnifier, a screen reader, a braille terminal, keyboard modifiers, and even an on-screen keyboard.

°   The real power and control over the boot process is available once you press the **F6** key. Here, you can see a menu of the common arguments that help the CD boot on difficult hardware. If you press the *Esc* key, you will move from this menu to the boot prompt. You can type extra kernel boot parameters that you might need for your hardware, as shown in the following screenshot:

```
                        ubuntu⊛




                    Install Ubuntu Server
              Multiple server install with MAAS
                   Check disc for defects
                        Test memory
                  Boot from first hard disk
                  Rescue a broken system




Boot Options  ireseed/ubuntu-server.seed vga=788 initrd=/install/initrd.gz quiet ---|

F1 Help  F2 Language  F3 Keymap  F4 Modes  F5 Accessibility  F6 Other Options
```

6.   Just after launching the installation process, you will be asked to choose the language of the installation procedure, which will be the default language of the server that you wish to install. Select the one that you want by using the up/down arrow keys on your keyboard and then press the *Enter* key. You will also be asked for the location of the server (based on this, the system will fix the server time settings). Then, you have a choice of either letting the installer detect your keyboard layout, or you entering it manually.

7. After performing these steps, the installer starts the installation process by detecting the hardware and loading some packages. Then, it moves on to configure the network settings by using **DHCP (Dynamic Host Configuration Protocol)** and asking for the hostname that you would like to give to your server. If you wouldn't like to use DHCP for network configuration, choose **go back** or simply press the *Esc* button to go to the first interface of network configuration, where you will find the **Configure the network manually** option, as shown in the following screenshot:

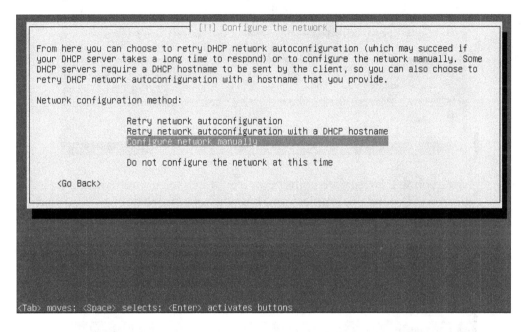

By making this choice, you will be asked via different interfaces to enter your IP address, Netmask, the default Gateway, and DNS.

Note that if you enter wrong information by mistake and you realize just after pressing the *Enter* key, don't worry. You can go back easily to the previous interface and re-enter the correct data. All that you need to do is choose **Go Back** or simply press the *Esc* button.

Also note that this data is not a tattoo, and you can change it later. We will have a look at how to do this in the next chapter.

8. At this point, we have almost finished the network settings part. We will be asked for the hostname in the next screen, and then we will move on to the user settings. First of all, you will be asked about the full username. Then, you will get an interface that asks for the Ubuntu username, which will be used for authentication with a proposition derived from the full username that you entered before. You can accept the proposition or modify it. Finally, you will be asked to enter and re-enter a password for this user. Be careful in this step because the keys entered will be hidden, as shown in the following screenshot. Therefore, it is important to remember the keys that you have entered:

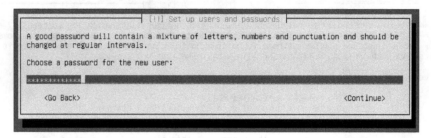

Next, you will be asked whether you would like to encrypt your home directory. Don't do that unless you know what you are doing. At the end of this step, you will be asked to check your time zone. Change it in case it is incorrect.

9. Now, the most critical part of the installation arrives — partitioning! If you are using a new hard disk, you will see a screen, as shown in the following screenshot:

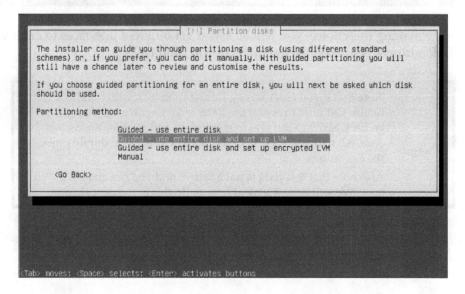

If you are using a used hard disk, you will receive an interface that is a little different. It contains in general the same four options with the options related to the reuse of the existing partitions. The first three options are the recommended ones for a newbie. In our case, we will choose the **Guided — use entire disk and set up LVM** option. The **Manual** option will be covered in the **Advanced installation** section.

On pressing the *Enter* key, you will be taken to the next screen, where you will be asked to choose the disk that you would like to partition. You will then be taken to an interface, which will ask for your permission to write changes on the disk with the **No** option selected. We of course need to make changes to the disk. We should just verify that we created a backup of our data on the disk before moving on. The next step is to select the **Yes** option and press the *Enter* key. Before you finish this step, you will be asked to enter the size of each volume group that you will be using for this partitioning. You can answer with a number followed by a symbol such as MB, GB, and TB, or simply use a percentage. Finally, you will get a summary of the partitioning step, which needs to be confirmed before it is applied, as shown in the following screenshot. Select the **Yes** option and press the *Enter* key:

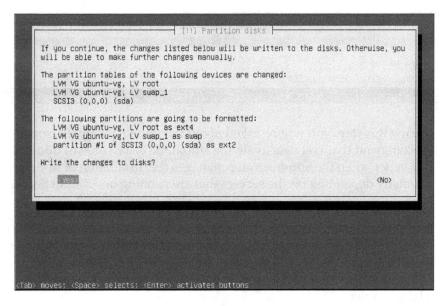

10. At this point, the real installation process starts. During the installation, the installer needs only the CD, but if there is an Internet connection, it can be used to download software lists and install the latest updates. For that, it will ask you to either enter the proxy settings if you have one, or to keep this field empty.

    After this step, the installer will start downloading the software list (we will cover this later in the next chapter). This step can take some time, depending on your Internet speed:

    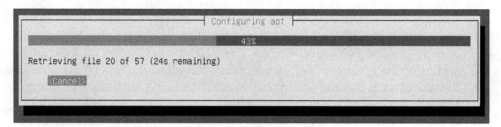

    After a few minutes, the installation process starts:

    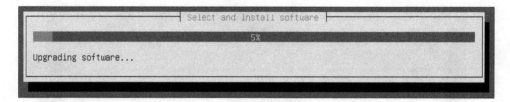

    During this step, you will be asked about the update policy. Personally, I recommend that you deactivate the automatic installation of updates. It is better when the administrator manages the installation of updates manually depending on the servers that are running on Ubuntu Server.

11. One of the useful facilities that are given by the Ubuntu installer is the ability to choose to install server packages such as the SSH and DNS server. You can choose one of them by pressing the *space bar*, and you can continue the installation process by pressing the *Enter* key. In our case, we will decide not to install a server at this step. We will have a look at how to do this in a later chapter:

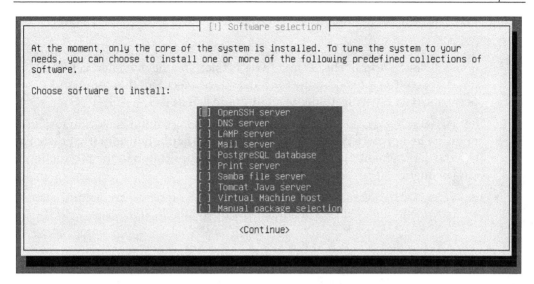

12. Finally, you will be asked to confirm the installation of the GRUB boot loader to the **Master Boot Recorder** (**MBR**). Then, you will get the following notification at the end of the installation process:

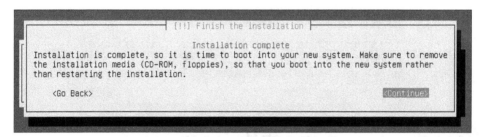

Upgrading from an old release

In case you have an existing Ubuntu Server and you would like to upgrade it to the newest release, you can use the `do-release-upgrade` command. This command is a part of the `update-manager-core` package; it does not have any graphical dependencies and is installed by default.

You can check the options list associated with this command by running the following:

```
do-release-upgrade --help
```

You will find the following options very useful:

- `do-release-upgrade --check-dist-upgrade-only`: The `--check-dist-upgrade-only` option checks for a new version. If a new version is found, it is displayed as a result in the terminal. Once executed, this command performs only a verification job; no upgrade is made.

- `do-release-upgrade --sandbox`: The `--sandbox` option is used to test an upgrade in a protected environment. This is particularly useful if you wish to test the deployment of an upgrade prior to its application in the production environment.

- `do-release-upgrade`: The `do-release-upgrade` tool researches and makes an upgrade to the next LTS or stable version available, if it exists.

> The upgrade policy used by the `do-release-upgrade` tool is defined in the `/etc/update-manager/release-upgrades` file. The prompt variable at the end of the file indicates whether only the LTS versions will be considered or all the versions (the LTS ones as well as the regular ones) will be searched for when asking for an upgrade. The prompt variable can take as values `lts` for the LTS versions, `normal` for all versions, and `never` to never search for new versions.
>
> You should only use the `Prompt=lts` mode when you are deploying a version of Ubuntu that is already an LTS. Otherwise, no new version will be detected by `do-release-upgrade`.

The advanced installation

Much of the Ubuntu Server installation process fulfils a majority of user needs, and it is used in the same manner by most of the users (newbie or advanced), but the part that requires much more attention and which is customized by many advanced system administrators depending on their needs is the partitioning step. In this section, we will have a look at how to perform an advanced partitioning for a specific hard disk schema.

Using RAID

The **RAID** technology (an acronym for **Redundant Array of Inexpensive Disks**) refers to the techniques used to distribute data across multiple hard drives (creating a storage unit from several hard disks). The unit thus created has an improved fault tolerance (high availability) or a greater performance (the capacity/write speed). The distribution of data on several hard drives allows you to increase the safety and reliability of the associated services.

 For more information about this technology, you can take a tour at `http://www.tldp.org/HOWTO/Software-RAID-HOWTO.html`.

In this section, we will see how to install Ubuntu Server using two RAID1 partitions on two different hard disks, one for the **root** and the other for **Swap**:

1. In the **Partition disk** step, select **manual**. Then, select one by one all the disks that you want and which should be a part of the RAID partitions (in our case, only two disks). For each disk, create a new empty partition table on it.

2. Select the free space on the first drive. Then, choose **Create a new partition**. Set the size that you want for **Swap**; it should be twice the RAM size and up to 2 GB. Then, choose **Primary** and select **Beginning**. The **physical volume for RAID** option should be chosen in the **Use as:** line. Finally, select **Done setting up partition**.

3. With the remaining free space, perform the same steps for the root partition. The only exception is that after setting the size, choose **Continue** and then select **Primary**. Also, select the **Bootable flag:** line to change the value to **on**.

4. Return to the **Partition Disks** step and select **Configure Software RAID** at the beginning of the page. Then, choose **yes** to write the modifications to disk.

5. In the **Create MD device** setup and for this example, choose **RAID1**, but if you are applying another architecture, choose the one that fits your needs.

6. Now, enter the number of hard drives that you have chosen for the array (in our case, we have two active devices). Then, select **Continue**.

7. Next, enter the number of spare devices (choose the default setting for RAID1, which is 0) and then select **Continue**.

8. At this step, choose the partitions that you wish to use. For the **Swap** partition, choose **sda1** and **sdb1**. Select **Continue** to go to the next step.

9. Repeat steps 3 to 7 to prepare the root partition, and at the end, choose **sda2** and **sdb2**. Finally, select **Finish**.

We should now have a list of RAID devices and hard drives. The next remaining steps are required to format and set the mount point for the RAID devices. Deal with the RAID devices as a local hard disk; format and mount accordingly:

1. Getting back to the initial partitioning page again, we will see our newly created **RAID devices #0** and **#1** partitions.

2. Under the **RAID1 device #0** partition, select **#1** and press the *Enter* key.

3. In the **Use as:** file, select **swap area** and then apply this partition by using the **Done setting up partition** entry.

4. Under the **RAID1 device #1** partition, select **#1** and press the *Enter* key.

5. In the **Use as:** file, select **Ext4 journaling file system**.

6. In the **Mount point** field, choose **/** (the root file system). You can change the other options as you wish. Then, apply that partition by using the **Done setting up partition** entry.

7. Finally, select **Finish partitioning and write changes to disk**.

The installation process will then continue normally.

Using LVM

LVM (Logical Volume Manager) allows the creation and the management of logical volume on Linux. The use of logical volumes somehow replaces the disks' partitioning. This is a much more flexible system as it allows you, for instance, to reduce the size of a file system to expand another one regardless of their location on disks.

 For more information about this technology, you can take a tour at `http://tldp.org/HOWTO/LVM-HOWTO/`.

In this section, we will have a look at the partitioning step of Ubuntu Server installation process with the **/srv** partition mounted on a LVM volume. This section will be divided into two parts—the first part is during the Ubuntu installation within only one **PV (physical volume)**, which will be a part of the **VG (volume group)**, and the second part will be after the Ubuntu installation. While performing this process, we will demonstrate how to add a second PV to the VG:

1. In the **Partition disks** screen, choose **Manual**.

2. Select the hard disk. Then, choose **Yes** to confirm the **Create a new empty partition table on this device** order.

3. Next, create standard swap and / partitions with the file system that you want.

4. For our /srv LVM partition, create a new logical partition and change the **Use as** field to **physical volume for LVM**. Then, select **Done setting up the partition**.

5. Now, choose **Configure the Logical Volume Manager** and select **Yes**.

6. On the next screen and for **LVM configuration action**, select **Create volume group**. Name the VG (for example, vg01). Then, select the partition prepared for LVM and choose **Continue**.

7. Return to the **LVM configuration action** page and select **Create logical volume**. Choose the newly created VG and name the new LV. Then, choose a size and at the end, select **Finish**. You will be taken to the main **Partition Disks** page again.

8. Now, let's add a file system to our new LVM. To do this, select the partition under the LVM that you created and set up the file system that you want and choose **/srv** as the mount point. Next, select **Done setting up the partition**.

9. Finally, apply the **Finish partitioning and write changes to disk** order. Then, confirm the changes and continue your installation.

Now, we will continue with the second part that started after the Ubuntu Server installation and which covers adding a second hard disk, creating a PV, adding it to the existing VG, extending LV with the srv command, and finally extending the file system. In this part, we will use a second hard disk named /dev/sdb, and we will use it entirely as a PV. You can configure and use as much of PV as you want:

1. First of all, create the PV using the following command:

```
sudo pvcreate /dev/sdb
```

2. Next, extend the VG (called vg01 in our example), as follows:

```
sudo vgextend vg01 /dev/sdb
```

3. Use the vgdisplay command to find out the size that you can allocate (for free physical extents, see the **Free PE / size** line). We will assume in our example a free size of 511 PE (which is equivalent to 2 GB with a size of 4 MB PE), and we will use the entire available free space.

4. We can now use the PE to extend the LV via the following command (there are other methods, but they are beyond the scope of this book):

```
sudo lvextend /dev/vg01/srv -l +511
```

5. We used the `-l` option here to extend the LV using PE. If you want to extend using MB, GB, and TB, you can use the `-l` option.

6. Before expanding an `ext3` or `ext4` file system, it is recommended that you unmount it before hand (as best practice). In case you want to reduce an LV, it will be mandatory to unmount it. The following commands unmount the partition and then check it:

```
sudo umount /srv
sudo e2fsck -f /dev/vg01/srv
```

7. Finally, you can resize the file system by using the following command:

```
sudo resize2fs /dev/vg01/srv
```

8. Now, you can mount the partition and check its new size using the following command:

```
mount /dev/vg01/srv /srv && df -h /srv
```

The automated installation

Sometimes, we have a large number of servers to install. In this case, the manual installation will take a lot of time to perform a repetitive task. To solve this problem, there is the automation installation, or what we call the network boot.

For this, we need a machine equipped with a DHCP server and a TFTP server that will provide us the services and configuration files that we need for the system to be installed.

The PXE process

The client computer (our future server) will boot its network interface in the **PXE** (**Preboot Execution Environment**) mode. Then, the DHCP present on the network will send it the `pxelinux.0` file; this will be explained later. Thus, the client computer accesses the `pxelinux.cfg` configuration file via TFTP, which contains the necessary information required to launch the installation process.

The PXE installation procedure

Let's start with the server installation:

1. First of all, install the DHCP server by using the `sudo apt-get install isc-dhcp-server -y` command, and then configure it by using the `/etc/default/isc-dhcp-server` file to use the network that you want for listening (such as `eth0`).

In the `/etc/dhcp/dhcpd.conf` file, you should configure some parameters such as the subnet and the address range. Then, restart it by using the following command:

```
sudo service isc-dhcp-server restart
```

2. After this, install the following packages that are necessary if you wish to set up the PXE environment:

```
sudo apt-get install apache2 tftpd-hpa inetutils-inetd
```

Now, it is time to configure the TFTP service. To do this, add the following two lines to the `/etc/default/tftpd-hpa` file:

```
RUN_DAEMON="yes"

OPTIONS="-l -s /var/lib/tftpboot"
```

Also, add the following line at the end of the `/etc/inetd.conf file`:

```
tftp    dgram    udp    wait    root    /usr/sbin/in.tftpd
/usr/sbin/in.tftpd -s /var/lib/tftpboot
```

Then, reboot the service using the `sudo /etc/init.d/tftpd-hpa restart` command.

3. Now, we need to copy the installation files to the PXE server. In our example, I used the ISO image that I have in my home directory. First of all, mount it by using the following command:

```
sudo mount loop /home/abdelmonam/ubuntu-15.04-server-amd64.iso
/mnt
```

Then, copy the required files to the server by using the following commands:

```
cd /mnt

sudo cp -fr install/netboot/* /var/lib/tftpboot/

sudo mkdir /var/www/Ubuntu

sudo cp -fr /mnt/* /var/www/ubuntu/
```

After doing this, modify the `/var/lib/tftpboot/pxelinux.cfg/default` PXE config file by adding the following lines at the end:

```
label linux

kernel ubuntu-installer/amd64/linux

append ks=http://192.168.1.1/ks.cfg vga=normal
initrd=ubuntu-installer/amd64/initrd.gz

ramdisk_size=16432 root=/dev/rd/0 rw  --
```

Be careful when adding the IP address.

4. The last step required to set up the PXE server is to add the following lines at the end of the `/etc/dhcp/dhcpd.conf` file:

```
allow booting;
allow bootp;
option option-128 code 128 = string;
option option-129 code 129 = text;
next-server 192.168.1.1;
filename "pxelinux.0";
```

Then, reboot the DHCP server by using the following command:

```
sudo service isc-dhcp-server restart
```

Let's move on to the client configuration. In our case, I used a `virtualbox` instance to test this kind of installation:

1. Create the virtual machine with the characteristics that you want via the `virtualbox` manager.

2. Then, go to the **Settings** of the machine and select the **System** tab. In the **Boot Order** part, deselect all options and select **Network**, as shown in the following screenshot:

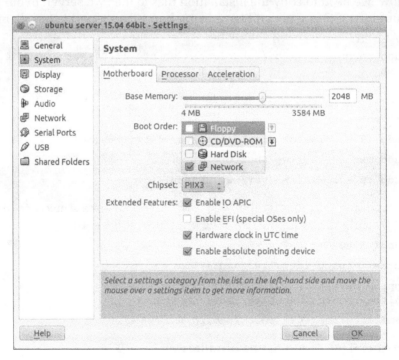

3. Select the **Network** tab and configure the network adaptor to act as a bridge.

4. Finally, start your VM. You will see the following interface:

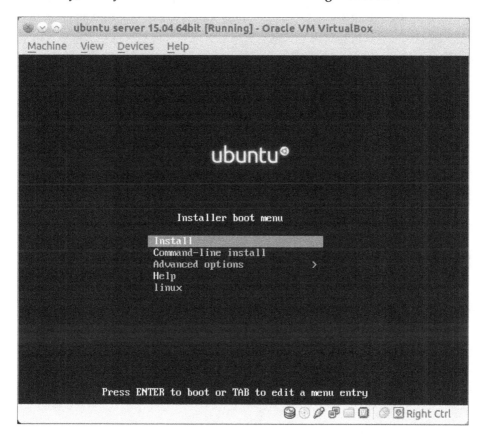

Enjoy watching the server installation if you were doing it locally from a CD.

> The PXE installation can be used to install a lot of machines in parallel as well as to install Ubuntu Server on machines without a CD-ROM driver.
>
> The installation process will be entirely automated if you combine the PXE method with a kickstart and/or preseed file. A good starting point for working with kickstart is https://help.ubuntu.com/community/KickstartCompatibility.

Additional resources

Since this book consists of the essentials for the Ubuntu Server, we can't cover topics in depth. Therefore, here are some useful links that will help you go as far as you want in this subject:

- For details regarding the installation of the Ubuntu desktop from a PXE server, visit `https://help.ubuntu.com/community/Installation/LocalNet`. You can use the same procedure to install Ubuntu Server.

- To learn how to prepare a PXE server that allows you to boot multiple distributions (Ubuntu, Debian, Fedora, CentOS, and openSUSE), visit `https://help.ubuntu.com/community/PXEInstallMultiDistro`.

- For those of you searching for how to set up a MAAS server that will deploy a Ubuntu system through `netboot`, a very good guide is available at `http://maas.ubuntu.com/docs/install.html`.

Summary

In this chapter, we had a look at how to install Ubuntu Server in different modes—manually and automated—with the help of a simple or an advanced installation.

Now, we can start managing our server, which is the subject that we will cover in the next chapter.

2

Configuring and Administering Ubuntu Server

After installing the Ubuntu Server, you will need to administrate it. If you are a newbie, this chapter is mandatory for you. So follow it to the letter. If you are an advanced Linux user who has experience working with other distributions, you can consider the experience of trying a new distribution similar to that of driving a new car. The car certainly has a steering wheel, a gas pedal, and a brake, but it still takes you a minute to adjust the mirrors, find out where the gauges and controls are, and adjust the seat until you feel comfortable. Think of this chapter as that minute or two behind the wheel of a new car.

To reach this goal, we will follow this plan:

- Administering using the command line
- The package management of an Ubuntu Server
- The network configuration for an Ubuntu Server
- Performing essential system administration tasks

Administering using the command line

Entire books have been written on command-line tools and how to use them effectively. In this section, we will have a look at the essentials one that we need. If you are an experienced administrator, feel free to skip to the next section. Just keep in mind the following note, that's all.

Note that unlike other Linux distributions, Ubuntu doesn't allow the use of the super user as a root by default; it is disabled for security reasons. So, when you would like to run a command with the root privileges, you should run it with the `sudo` keyword before doing so. You will be asked to enter your password (the one that you used when installing the Ubuntu Server). For example, if you would like to edit the `/etc/hosts` file, run the following code:

```
abdelmonam@abdelmonam-tactic:~$ sudo vi /etc/hosts
[sudo] password for abdelmonam:
```

If you would like to activate the root account (which is not recommended) or allow other users to run `sudo`, you can follow the detailed tutorial at. `https://help.ubuntu.com/community/RootSudo`.

Now, let's start with what I consider to be the most important command for a Linux administrator — man, or the interface for online reference manuals. It gives you the necessary information about any command that you would like to use (if it is documented of course, which is true in most cases). We use it by typing the man keyword just before the command that we would like to be informed about. We use arrows keys to navigate, the / character to perform a search, the *Enter* key to view the next line, the *spacebar* to view the next page, and the *q* character to quit the interface. For example, the following screenshot shows what you will see when you run the man ls command:

```
LS(1)                          User Commands                          LS(1)

NAME
       ls - list directory contents

SYNOPSIS
       ls [OPTION]... [FILE]...

DESCRIPTION
       List  information  about  the FILEs (the current directory by default).
       Sort entries alphabetically if none of -cftuvSUX nor --sort  is  speci■
       fied.

       Mandatory  arguments  to  long  options are mandatory for short options
       too.

       -a, --all
              do not ignore entries starting with .

       -A, --almost-all
              do not list implied . and ..

       --author
              with -l, print the author of each file
Manual page ls(1) line 1 (press h for help or q to quit)
```

The man pages are grouped together in sections, with one section per topic. For example, the man pages in the first section are executable programs or shell commands, the ones in section 2 are **system calls** (functions provided by the kernel), and so on. You can see all the sections on running the man man command.

Another useful command is apropos, which shows the section and man page where the word in the parameter was found. For example, when searching the man pages/ sections in which the pwd command exists, we use the following command:

```
abdelmonam@abdelmonam-tactic:~$ apropos pwd
lckpwdf (3)             - get shadow password file entry
pwd (1)                 - print name of current/working directory
pwdx (1)                - report current working directory of a process
ulckpwdf (3)            - get shadow password file entry
unix_chkpwd (8)         - Helper binary that verifies the password of
the current user
```

Let's consider a case where a command exists under more than one section, as follows:

```
abdelmonam@abdelmonam-tactic:~$ apropos smbpasswd
smbpasswd (5)           - The Samba encrypted password file
smbpasswd (8)           - change a user's SMB password
```

You can view the information related to this section by using man <the_section_ number> <the_command> (for example, man 5 smbpasswd). Alternatively, use man -a <the_command> if you would like to see all the man page sections in succession for that command (for example, man -a smbpasswd). If you omit the section number, man will return the man page from the first section that it finds.

The ls command lists files and directories under the path passed in the parameter (the actual . directory is the default choice). Some options are very helpful. For example, with the -a option, we can list the cached items. With the -l option, we can get additional information such as the file size and permissions:

```
abdelmonam@abdelmonam-tactic:~$ ls -la /etc/systemd/
total 48
drwxr-xr-x  5 root root 4096 Jun  2 17:30 .
drwxr-xr-x 93 root root 4096 Jun  2 17:40 ..
-rw-r--r--  1 root root  720 Apr 18 22:11 bootchart.conf
-rw-r--r--  1 root root  970 Apr 18 22:11 journald.conf
-rw-r--r--  1 root root  966 Apr 18 22:11 logind.conf
drwxr-xr-x  2 root root 4096 Apr 18 22:11 network
```

```
-rw-r--r--  1 root root  589 Apr 18 22:11 resolved.conf
drwxr-xr-x 13 root root 4096 Jun  2 17:38 system
-rw-r--r--  1 root root 1471 Apr 18 22:11 system.conf
-rw-r--r--  1 root root  607 Apr 18 22:11 timesyncd.conf
drwxr-xr-x  2 root root 4096 Apr 18 22:11 user
-rw-r--r--  1 root root 1127 Apr 18 22:11 user.conf
```

The pwd command gives the current path (working directory).

The history command lists the last commands that you ran.

The chmod command allows you to change file permissions. Use it carefully, especially when you use the * magic card instead of a filename coupled with the -R option that runs it recursively. From the same family, we will find the chown and chgrp commands, which allow you to change the owner and group of a file respectively.

The top command gives you a list of the processes that are running on your Ubuntu Server; they are sorted by the CPU usage. This list is updated in real time, and it is limited by the size of the screen. If you want to see the whole list of the processes that are running on the system, you can run the famous ps -ef | less command. Here, we pipe the result of this command by using the | character as an input to the less command to see the result output page by page, less works like the famous more command. Besides, it allows you to surf forward and backward.

> Note that piping (using the | character) is a mechanism used to optimize commands output by passing the output of the first command (the command before the | character) as an input to the second command (the command after the | character). We can use a cascade of pipes using the | character in a single command line.

There are some useful shortcuts in the server environment (no graphic interface), such as *Ctrl+C*, which is used to quit a command that is not responding (or is simply taking too long to complete), *Ctrl+D*, which is used to send the **end of file** (**EOF**) signal to a command, and finally *Ctrl+Z*, which is used to stop the command that is running in the foreground (on the console). Even though it does stop the command, it does not terminate it. Instead, it is just paused. We can resume it easily either in the background via the bg command or again in the foreground with the fg command. To do this, you need the job number associated with the program that you want to start again. You can get a list of the job numbers by using the jobs command.

For file management, you will need to use `mkdir` for directory creation, `cd` to enter a directory, `touch` to create a file, and `cat` to view its contents. For directory/file management, you can use `cp` for copy, `rm` for remove, and `mv` for move/rename.

To edit a file, you can use either of the two famous editors, `vi` or `vim`.

Note that these are the most useful CLI commands. In the following sections and chapters in this book, we will have a look at other commands. An explanation for each of the commands will be given every time we need them. In case you would like to take advantage of a specific command, you can use the `man` command, as seen previously.

If you would like to learn more about Linux **command line (CLI)**, I recommend that you refer to the book available at `http://linuxcommand.org/tlcl.php`.

It is mandatory to know the basics of the `vi`/`vim` editors when you are working in a server environment. Learning how to use `vi` is beyond the scope of this book. So, you have to make some effort to do it yourself. For more help, you can find good basic training for the `vi` editor at `http://www.cs.colostate.edu/helpdocs/vi.html`.

The package management for an Ubuntu Server

Ubuntu, like other Debian-based systems, uses the Debian package format, such as `.deb` packages. I prefer using a `.deb` package when installing software instead of `tarball` archives because on one hand, unlike the case with `tarball`, we can get traceability for every piece of software installed on your system with `.deb` packages. On the other hand, because only a `.deb` package can request the package database on your server via the package manager and get information about the installed and available packages on your system, the package manager takes care of installing the missing dependencies automatically.

Package repositories

Ubuntu packages exist in repositories, which are collections of packages, in a pre-compiled binary format that can be located either on different medias, such as CD-ROMs, or on the Internet. There are four official repositories provided by Canonical (the company that created Ubuntu):

- `main`: This is the repository that contains software distributed under a completely free license and supported by the Ubuntu team.
- `restricted`: This is the repository that contains software that may not be under a completely free license but is supported by the Ubuntu team, such as drivers for specific hardware components.
- `universe`: This repository contains most of the open source software available in the Linux world and which exists under licenses that may not be as free as the others. Software in this repository is not supported by the Ubuntu team.
- `multiverse`: Here, you will find software that does not meet the free concept standards of software. Software in this repository is not supported by the Ubuntu team.

There are a lot of other repositories. Many of them are owned by software editors and contain packages related to their products. Most of them are provided by the community and exist under the **Personal Package Archives (PPA)** which is a repository software for Ubuntu (visit `https://launchpad.net/ubuntu/+ppas` for more information).

The managing of repositories on your Ubuntu Server is done in the `/etc/apt/sources.list` file. Here's a sample of this file from a fresh Ubuntu Server installation:

```
abdelmonam@abdelmonam-tactic:~$ cat /etc/apt/sources.list
#

# deb cdrom:[Ubuntu-Server 15.04 _Vivid Vervet_ - Release amd64
(20150422)]/ vivid main restricted

#deb cdrom:[Ubuntu-Server 15.04 _Vivid Vervet_ - Release amd64
(20150422)]/ vivid main restricted

# See http://help.ubuntu.com/community/UpgradeNotes for how to
upgrade to
# newer versions of the distribution.
deb http://tn.archive.ubuntu.com/ubuntu/ vivid main restricted
deb-src http://tn.archive.ubuntu.com/ubuntu/ vivid main restricted
```

```
## Major bug fix updates produced after the final release of the
## distribution.
deb http://tn.archive.ubuntu.com/ubuntu/ vivid-updates main
restricted
deb-src http://tn.archive.ubuntu.com/ubuntu/ vivid-updates main
restricted


## N.B. software from this repository is ENTIRELY UNSUPPORTED by the
Ubuntu
## team. Also, please note that software in universe WILL NOT receive
any
## review or updates from the Ubuntu security team.
deb http://tn.archive.ubuntu.com/ubuntu/ vivid universe
deb-src http://tn.archive.ubuntu.com/ubuntu/ vivid universe
deb http://tn.archive.ubuntu.com/ubuntu/ vivid-updates universe
deb-src http://tn.archive.ubuntu.com/ubuntu/ vivid-updates universe


## N.B. software from this repository is ENTIRELY UNSUPPORTED by the
Ubuntu
## team, and may not be under a free licence. Please satisfy yourself
as to
## your rights to use the software. Also, please note that software
in
## multiverse WILL NOT receive any review or updates from the Ubuntu
## security team.
deb http://tn.archive.ubuntu.com/ubuntu/ vivid multiverse
deb-src http://tn.archive.ubuntu.com/ubuntu/ vivid multiverse
deb http://tn.archive.ubuntu.com/ubuntu/ vivid-updates multiverse
deb-src http://tn.archive.ubuntu.com/ubuntu/ vivid-updates multiverse


## N.B. software from this repository may not have been tested as
## extensively as that contained in the main release, although it
includes
## newer versions of some applications which may provide useful
features.
## Also, please note that software in backports WILL NOT receive any
review
## or updates from the Ubuntu security team.
```

```
deb http://tn.archive.ubuntu.com/ubuntu/ vivid-backports main
restricted universe multiverse
deb-src http://tn.archive.ubuntu.com/ubuntu/ vivid-backports main
restricted universe multiverse


deb http://security.ubuntu.com/ubuntu vivid-security main restricted
deb-src http://security.ubuntu.com/ubuntu vivid-security main
restricted
deb http://security.ubuntu.com/ubuntu vivid-security universe
deb-src http://security.ubuntu.com/ubuntu vivid-security universe
deb http://security.ubuntu.com/ubuntu vivid-security multiverse
deb-src http://security.ubuntu.com/ubuntu vivid-security multiverse


## Uncomment the following two lines to add software from Canonical's
## 'partner' repository.
## This software is not part of Ubuntu, but is offered by Canonical
and the
## respective vendors as a service to Ubuntu users.
# deb http://archive.canonical.com/ubuntu vivid partner
# deb-src http://archive.canonical.com/ubuntu vivid partner
```

After modifying the sources list file, update the packages database using the `sudo apt-get update` command. We will have a look at how to work with the `apt` tool in the next section.

Package management utilities

In Ubuntu, there are a few package management utilities, especially in a non-graphical environment such as those of most server installations. In the following section, you will discover the three most used tools — `dpkg`, `aptitude` and `apt` — besides the famous `tasksel` utility.

 Note that working with more than one package management database can be confusing. I recommend that you choose one package management system to work with and stick to it. For the rest of this book, we will use `apt`.

The dpkg tool

This tool is used to manage (install, remove, and build) local .deb packages from a CD-ROM or some other disk storage. It doesn't automatically download and install packages from repositories and manage dependencies.

The dpkg tool is powerful. It can be used when working with locally installed packages. For example, it helps you list all the packages installed on your system, even the ones installed with other utilities, such as apt. To see that, you should run the command dpkg -l (because the output of this command is a huge list you can run dpkg -l command less to check them page per page). The following is the result of dpkg -l | less on our server:

```
Desired=Unknown/Install/Remove/Purge/Hold
| Status=Not/Inst/Conf-files/Unpacked/halF-conf/Half-inst/trig-aWait/Trig-pend
|/ Err?=(none)/Reinst-required (Status,Err: uppercase=bad)
||/ Name                      Version                      Architectur
e Description
+++-=============================-===========================-============
=-=========================================================-============
=
ii  accountsservice          0.6.37-1ubuntu10            amd64
    query and manipulate user account information
ii  acpid                     1:2.0.23-1ubuntu1           amd64
    Advanced Configuration and Power Interface event daemon
ii  adduser                   3.113+nmu3ubuntu3           all
    add and remove users and groups
ii  apparmor                  2.9.1-0ubuntu9              amd64
    User-space parser utility for AppArmor
ii  apport                    2.17.2-0ubuntu1             all
    automatically generate crash reports for debugging
ii  apport-symptoms           0.20                        all
    symptom scripts for apport
ii  apt                       1.0.9.7ubuntu4              amd64
    commandline package manager
ii  apt-transport-https       1.0.9.7ubuntu4              amd64
    https download transport for APT
:
```

The dpkg command can also list the different files installed with a specific package. In this case, we should use the -l option, with the name of the package as a parameter. As shown in the following screenshot, we listed the files installed with the isc-dhcp-common package:

```
ubuntu@abdelmonam-tactic:~$ dpkg -L isc-dhcp-common
/.
/usr
/usr/bin
/usr/bin/omshell
/usr/share
/usr/share/doc
/usr/share/doc/isc-dhcp-common
/usr/share/doc/isc-dhcp-common/copyright
/usr/share/doc/isc-dhcp-common/changelog.Debian.gz
/usr/share/man
/usr/share/man/man1
/usr/share/man/man1/omshell.1.gz
/usr/share/man/man5
/usr/share/man/man5/dhcp-options.5.gz
/usr/share/man/man5/dhcp-eval.5.gz
ubuntu@abdelmonam-tactic:~$ _
```

On the other hand, we can check for a specific file within the package that it was installed in by using the -S option. As shown in the following screenshot, the /usr/bin/omshell file was installed with the isc-dhcp-common package:

```
ubuntu@abdelmonam-tactic:~$ dpkg -S /usr/bin/omshell
isc-dhcp-common: /usr/bin/omshell
```

 Note that many files are automatically generated during package installation, and even though they are on the file system, dpkg -S may not know which package they belong to.

With dpkg, we can install the local .deb packages by using the -i option:

```
sudo dpkg -i <file_name.deb>
```

We can also remove packages by using the -r option, but it is not recommended because dpkg doesn't handle dependencies. If you use dpkg to remove a specific package that one or more programs depend on, you may break those programs.

The aptitude tool

The aptitude tool is based on **apt** (**Advanced Packaging Tool**), which will be discussed later in this chapter, but this tool is more user-friendly. You can use aptitude either with the search keyword to search for a specific word in the package description database, or with the show keyword to display a lot of useful information about a specific package. However, the most helpful use of aptitude is that you can launch it without a keyword and you will get a menu-driven text-based frontend for apt. This interface is suitable for server environments (usually non graphical tool). It helps users perform a lot of tasks automatically.

When you execute the sudo aptitude command, you will see the following interface:

```
 Actions   Undo   Package   Resolver   Search   Options   Views   Help
C-T: Menu   ?: Help   q: Quit   u: Update   g: Download/Install/Remove Pkgs
aptitude 0.6.11

--- Upgradable Packages (12)
--- Installed Packages (459)
--- Not Installed Packages (75254)
--- Virtual Packages (10551)
--- Tasks (60624)




Security updates for these packages are available from security.ubuntu.com.

This group contains 12 packages.
```

You can view the `Package` menu by using the *Ctrl+T* shortcut and navigate by using the arrow keys, as shown in the following screenshot:

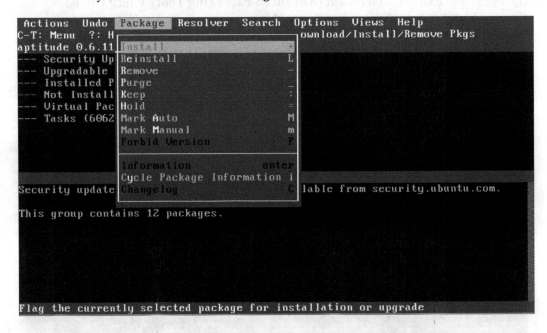

You can also use `aptitude` as a command-line interface (a non-menu-driven interface) in a way that is similar to how you use `apt` as a command-line interface. For example, you can use `sudo aptitude install bind9` to install the `bind9` DNS server.

The apt tools

The `apt` is used to download and install packages from online repositories. The `apt` commands (`apt-get`, `apt-cache`, and so on) are normally used to work with online software. However, they can also be used to install packages locally.

The `apt-cache` command allows you to manipulate the apt package cache. The `apt-cache` command does not modify the state of the system, but it does provide functions with which to search and generate useful output from the package metadata. For example, with the `search` keyword, you can search for a word in the package description database. With the `show` keyword, you can show the details of a specific package.

The `apt-get` tool is powerful. It performs a lot of functions, such as installing new package, upgrading an old package, updating the package database, and even upgrading the entire Ubuntu Server.

To install a new package, all you need to do is run the package with the `install` keyword. For example, to install the `apache2` web server, you should run the following command:

```
sudo apt-get install apache2
```

You can of course remove it using the following command:

```
sudo apt-get remove apache2
```

 Note that with the `--purge` option, you can also remove configuration files. So use it carefully.

We can install and remove a whole list of packages at the same time. Just write the packages' names, with the names separated by spaces.

A common use of `apt-get` is updating a software database after the modification of the source list file. To do this, execute the following command:

```
sudo apt-get update
```

Over time, a lot of packages will have newer versions. Therefore, an `upgrade` operation is needed to keep your Ubuntu Server up-to-date, especially when talking about security updates. The `apt-get` tool allows us to do this by using the following command (after updating the database, as discussed before):

```
sudo apt-get upgrade.
```

 Note that in general, after a new installation, the first thing that we need to do is upgrade all the software of the system by running the following command:
```
sudo apt-get update && sudo apt-get upgrade
```

For more information about `apt-get`, you can refer to the man pages or use the `help` keyword, as shown in the following code:

```
abdelmonam@abdelmonam-tactic:~$ apt-get help
apt 1.0.9.7ubuntu4 for amd64 compiled on Apr  7 2015 14:42:59
Usage: apt-get [options] command
   apt-get [options] install|remove pkg1 [pkg2 ...]
   apt-get [options] source pkg1 [pkg2 ...]
```

apt-get is a simple command line interface for downloading and installing packages. The most frequently used commands are update and install.

Commands:
  update - Retrieve new lists of packages
  upgrade - Perform an upgrade
  install - Install new packages (pkg is libc6 not libc6.deb)
  remove - Remove packages
  autoremove - Remove automatically all unused packages
  purge - Remove packages and config files
  source - Download source archives
  build-dep - Configure build-dependencies for source packages
  dist-upgrade - Distribution upgrade, see apt-get(8)
  dselect-upgrade - Follow dselect selections
  clean - Erase downloaded archive files
  autoclean - Erase old downloaded archive files
  check - Verify that there are no broken dependencies
  changelog - Download and display the changelog for the given
package
  download - Download the binary package into the current directory

Options:
  -h This help text.
  -q Loggable output - no progress indicator
  -qq No output except for errors
  -d Download only - do NOT install or unpack archives
  -s No-act. Perform ordering simulation
  -y Assume Yes to all queries and do not prompt
  -f Attempt to correct a system with broken dependencies in place
  -m Attempt to continue if archives are unlocatable
  -u Show a list of upgraded packages as well
  -b Build the source package after fetching it
  -V Show verbose version numbers
  -c=? Read this configuration file

```
 -o=? Set an arbitrary configuration option, eg -o dir::cache=/tmp
See the apt-get(8), sources.list(5) and apt.conf(5) manual
pages for more information and options.
This APT has Super Cow Powers.
```

Adding software collections using tasksel

The `tasksel` tool provides you with the possibility of installing new software and configuring them at the same time—either by using default values, or by asking you to enter the appropriate values. As a result, you will get the software that you want to install working and ready to use without any need for additional customization (you can of course reconfigure it as you want later).

You may remember that during the installation of software, we saw an interface that which asked us to install some servers (such as DNS, mail, web, and so on). This task can be accomplished with the help of `tasksel`. We can launch the same menu interface at any time by using the following command:

`sudo tasksel`

The output of this command is as follows:

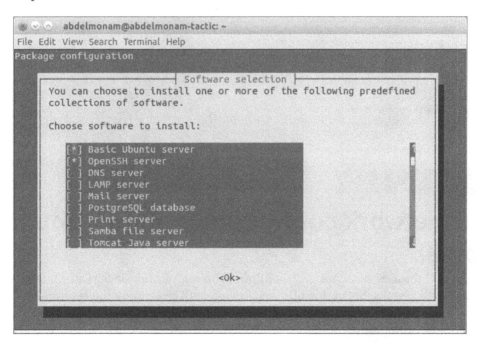

Use the arrow keys to navigate between the collections, press the *spacebar* to select the software that you want to install (you will see an asterisk to the left of the software), press the *Tab* key to navigate to the **OK** button, and press the *Enter* key to launch the installation.

If you would like to know which packages will be installed for a specific task, you can run, for the example of the lamp web server, the following command:

```
abdelmonam@abdelmonam-tactic:~$ tasksel --task-packages lamp-server
libmysqlclient18
apache2
php5-cli
libapache2-mod-php5
apache2.2-common
apache2-utils
php5-common
php5-mysql
mysql-server
apache2.2-bin
mysql-client-5.5
mysql-server-5.5
perl-modules
perl
mysql-server-core-5.5
mysql-client-core-5.5
ssl-cert
apache2-mpm-prefork
mysql-common
```

The network configuration for an Ubuntu Server

To cover all the aspects of network configuration for a Linux system administrator, we need huge books. So, in this little section, we will cover only the essential topics that every Ubuntu Server administrator will need to set up and change the network settings.

The configuration files

In this section, we will have a look at the core files for the network settings for the Ubuntu Server.

 Note that after modifying any of these files, you should restart the network process by typing in the following command:

`sudo /etc/init.d/networking restart`

Unlike Red Hat manners, Ubuntu and all the Debian-based distributions use a unique file to configure all the network interfaces; this file is named `/etc/network/interfaces`. In general, for Ubuntu servers, you will find the loopback and Ethernet interfaces. For loopback interfaces (127.0.0.1), its configuration is standard and doesn't need any modification from your side. For Ethernet interfaces, you will (in most of the cases when you are dealing with servers) find more than one interface. They are generally named `ethX`, where `X` is a number starting from `0` and which is incremented according to the interface number.

An Ethernet interface is configured in either the DHCP or static mode. If it is the DHCP mode, we will find the following lines in `/etc/network/interfaces`:

```
auto eth0
iface eth0 inet dhcp
```

Here, the line containing the `auto` keyword means that this interface should be automatically brought up when a computer boots up.

If it is in the static mode, you will find the output that looks like the following lines:

```
iface eth0 inet static
address 192.168.1.58
netmask 255.255.255.0
gateway 192.168.1.1
```

These fields are simple and pretty self-explanatory.

Another important network configuration file is `/etc/resolv.conf`, which contains the DNS list used by your server. If you are using DHCP, the content of this file will be set automatically. You can edit it by adding your own/favorite DNS servers in the following format:

```
nameserver 192.168.1.11
nameserver 192.168.1.12
```

The order of the DNS servers in this list will be followed when processing a DNS request.

 Note that in general, we edit DNS servers using the following command:

```
sudo vi /etc/resolv.conf
```

However, starting from Ubuntu 12.04 and later, you should use the following:

```
sudo vi /etc/resolvconf/resolv.conf.d/base
```

The /etc/hosts file is also one of the core network setting files. By default, it contains the loopback and local host addresses, but you can add to it another address/hostname pair. It will be used before checking the DNS. It is also useful when you want to assign an IP address to a hostname even if your DNS is down. This file is also used by a lot of services. We will have a look at this in the next chapter.

The network utilities

In this section, we will take a look at a set of networking programs that an administrator on an Ubuntu Server should be aware of.

The first two that you should know about are ifup and ifdown, which are used to put up interfaces and take them down respectively. You should use them with the name of the interface in the parameter.

Be careful when you take down an interface. You may potentially disrupt any services on the system. Furthermore, if you are connected to the system via SSH and you take down the main interface on the system, you will disconnect yourself from SSH.

Another important tool is ifconfig, which gives you detailed information about interfaces, as follows:

```
abdelmonam@abdelmonam-tactic:~$ ifconfig
eth0    Link encap:Ethernet   HWaddr 08:00:27:74:26:9b
        inet addr:192.168.1.58  Bcast:192.168.1.255  Mask:255.255.255.0
        inet6 addr: fe80::a00:27ff:fe74:269b/64 Scope:Link
        UP BROADCAST RUNNING MULTICAST  MTU:1500  Metric:1
        RX packets:3182 errors:0 dropped:0 overruns:0 frame:0
```

```
         TX packets:758 errors:0 dropped:0 overruns:0 carrier:0

         collisions:0 txqueuelen:1000

         RX bytes:296560 (296.5 KB)  TX bytes:117994 (117.9 KB)


lo       Link encap:Local Loopback

         inet addr:127.0.0.1  Mask:255.0.0.0

         inet6 addr: ::1/128 Scope:Host

         UP LOOPBACK RUNNING  MTU:65536  Metric:1

         RX packets:176 errors:0 dropped:0 overruns:0 frame:0

         TX packets:176 errors:0 dropped:0 overruns:0 carrier:0

         collisions:0 txqueuelen:0

         RX bytes:14144 (14.1 KB)  TX bytes:14144 (14.1 KB)
```

The `ifconfig` command also allows you to configure interfaces, put them up, and take them down. You can take a look at its potential via `man ifconfig`.

Another important networking program is the `route` command. As with `ifconfig`, this command can be used to both see and set network settings (network routes in this case). It is used to manage routes on your server (such as to list, add, remove, and so on). Let's take a look at the following command:

```
abdelmonam@abdelmonam-tactic:~$ route

Kernel IP routing table

Destination  Gateway      Genmask          Flags Metric Ref    Use Iface

default      192.168.1.1  0.0.0.0          UG    0      0        0 eth0

192.168.1.0  *            255.255.255.0 U         0      0        0 eth0
```

In the same context of routing configuration, there is the famous `traceroute6` command, which gives you the path followed by packets `egressing` from your server until their destination.

The `ethtool` command is a program that manipulates the Ethernet card settings, such as port speed, auto-negotiation, the duplex mode, and Wake-on-LAN. You can install it by using the following command:

```
sudo apt-get install ethtool
```

To check the `ethtool` options, you have to run either `man ethtool` or `ethtool -h | less`.

Performing essential system administration tasks

In this section, we will explore a useful set of Ubuntu Server administration tasks such as monitoring and processes management.

Monitoring resources

For a system administrator, monitoring tasks are the most important because they allow us to keep our system robust and prevent incidents. The Ubuntu Server has a powerful set of monitoring tools that cover CPU usage, hard disks, virtual memory, and so on.

Some tools come with Ubuntu straight out of the box, while others need to be installed. The `sysstat` package contains some of them. You need to install it by using the command:

```
sudo apt-get install sysstat
```

One of the most important resources that an Ubuntu Server administrator should permanently monitor is the memory use, because running out of memory will negatively affect system performance.

You can use the `free` and `top` commands to see basic information about the use of your RAM and swap. To get more detailed information about your server memory use, you can refer to the `vmstat` command. The `slabtop` command is useful in case you would like to show how much memory the kernel (the slab cache) of your server is consuming.

As seen earlier, the `top` command is used to watch the currently running processes. By default, those processes are sorted by the CPU usage. You can also use `top` to keep a tab on your memory usage in a screen-oriented way. When top is running, just press *Shift+m*, and the running processes will be sorted by the memory use (so that you can examine which processes are consuming memory the most).

Another important system resource that an Ubuntu Server administrator monitors is the CPU usage. The `vmstat` command that we previously talked about can produce basic statistics related to CPU usage, such as system activity, user activity, the I/O wait time, the idle time, and so on. If you want more detailed reports of CPU utilization, you can use the `iostat` command that comes with the `sysstat` package, which was installed at the beginning of this section.

For example, here's how the CPU statistics are shown every 5 seconds:

```
abdelmonam@abdelmonam-tactic:~$ iostat -c 5
Linux 3.19.0-15-generic (abdelmonam-tactic)   2015-06-13   _x86_64_
  (1 CPU)


avg-cpu:  %user   %nice  %system  %iowait  %steal   %idle
          24,27   0,08    5,17     0,94     0,00    69,55


avg-cpu:  %user   %nice %system %iowait  %steal   %idle
          24,45   0,00   3,41    0,25     0,00    71,89


avg-cpu:  %user   %nice %system %iowait  %steal   %idle
          24,66   0,00    3,11    0,15    0,00    72,08


avg-cpu:  %user   %nice %system %iowait  %steal   %idle
          28,17   0,00   3,39    0,10     0,00    68,34


avg-cpu:  %user   %nice %system %iowait  %steal   %idle
          23,97   0,00   2,65    0,41     0,00    72,98


avg-cpu:  %user   %nice %system %iowait  %steal   %idle
          25,08   0,00   3,13    0,21     0,00    71,59


avg-cpu:  %user   %nice %system %iowait  %steal   %idle
          25,56   0,00   3,46    0,00     0,00    70,99
```

An alternative to `iostat` in terms of viewing CPU usage information as well as other performance-related items is the `dstat` command, which comes with the `dstat` package. The `dstat` command has some advantages over other tools, such as the simplicity and clarity of information shown, and the use of colors. To install this tool, install the `dstat` package using the following command:

```
$ sudo apt-get install dstat
```

Here is an example of `dstat` displaying CPU information:

```
abdelmonam@abdelmonam-tactic: ~
File Edit View Search Terminal Help
abdelmonam@abdelmonam-tactic:~$ dstat -t -c 3
---system--- ---total-cpu-usage----
     time     |usr sys idl wai hiq siq
13-06 17:32:56| 24   5  70   1   0   0
13-06 17:32:59| 28   3  68   0   0   0
13-06 17:33:02| 29   3  68   0   0   0
13-06 17:33:05| 30   4  66   0   0   0
13-06 17:33:08| 27   3  70   0   0   0
13-06 17:33:11| 24   4  71   1   0   0
13-06 17:33:14| 25   3  71   0   0   0
13-06 17:33:17| 24   3  73   0   0   0
13-06 17:33:20| 24   3  73   0   0   0
13-06 17:33:23| 23   3  74   0   0   0
13-06 17:33:24| 30   3  66   1   0   0
```

As discussed previously, the `top` command allows you to specifically find out which processes are consuming processing time the most. By default, the sorting order is based on CPU usage, but if you change it for some reason (like we did before when we changed it so that it was based on memory usage), you can revert to the default sorting order by using the *Shift+p* command when `top` is running.

Commands such as `du` and `df` allow you get basic information about storage space available to your Ubuntu Server. For more details about how your storage devices are performing, you can use commands such as `vmstat` and `iostat`.

Let's have a look at the capacity of the `vmstat` command by using it to list statistics related to your disks. Here's an example of using `vmstat` to view information about the disk read and write statistics using the -d option:

abdelmonam@abdelmonam-tactic:~$ vmstat -d

disk	-------reads--------				---------writes--------			-----IO------		
	total	merged	sectors	ms	total	merged	sectors	ms	cur	sec
ram0	0	0	0	0	0	0	0	0	0	0
ram1	0	0	0	0	0	0	0	0	0	0
ram2	0	0	0	0	0	0	0	0	0	0

ram3	0	0	0	0	0	0	0	0	0	0
ram4	0	0	0	0	0	0	0	0	0	0
ram5	0	0	0	0	0	0	0	0	0	0
ram6	0	0	0	0	0	0	0	0	0	0
ram7	0	0	0	0	0	0	0	0	0	0
ram8	0	0	0	0	0	0	0	0	0	0
ram9	0	0	0	0	0	0	0	0	0	0
ram10	0	0	0	0	0	0	0	0	0	0
ram11	0	0	0	0	0	0	0	0	0	0
ram12	0	0	0	0	0	0	0	0	0	0
ram13	0	0	0	0	0	0	0	0	0	0
ram14	0	0	0	0	0	0	0	0	0	0
ram15	0	0	0	0	0	0	0	0	0	0
loop0	0	0	0	0	0	0	0	0	0	0
loop1	0	0	0	0	0	0	0	0	0	0
loop2	0	0	0	0	0	0	0	0	0	0
loop3	0	0	0	0	0	0	0	0	0	0
loop4	0	0	0	0	0	0	0	0	0	0
loop5	0	0	0	0	0	0	0	0	0	0
loop6	0	0	0	0	0	0	0	0	0	0
loop7	0	0	0	0	0	0	0	0	0	0
sr0	0	0	0	0	0	0	0	0	0	0
sr1	0	0	0	0	0	0	0	0	0	0
sda	6742	89	493438	73140	732	969	43336	17552	0	37

Another useful command in terms of file system management is lsof. It allows you to find out what files and directories are actually open on your storage devices. One of the most common cases where you need to use this command is when you are trying to unmount a file system that keeps telling you that it is busy. In this case, you can evaluate which open file is preventing the unmounting, decide if you want to stop the process holding that file open, and perform the unmounting of the file system again.

Processes management

As discussed before, the ps and top commands allow us to show a lot of information related to the running processes. In this section, we will examine other commands that allow us to manage processes.

When you are running top, you can perform a lot of actions besides sorting. For example, you can type the letter *k* followed by a signal number (for example, 9 or 15) and the PID, which sends that signal to the process that has this PID. You can also use the letter *n* to change the priority of one process.

Another way to change the priority of a running process is via the `renice` command. If you want to change the default priority or set a higher or lower priority at the time of launching a process, you can use the nice command.

Another way that can be used to change how a running process behaves is to send a signal to that process. Commands such as `kill`, `pkill`, and `killall` can be used to send signals to running processes. We can represent signals by numbers (the famous ones are 9 and 15) and strings (such as SIGKILL and SIGTERM).

Scheduling the processes that need to be run

Commands associated with the `cron` facility can be used to make a command run at a specific time (including now) so that it is not connected to the current shell. The `at` command runs a command at the time you set. For example, if you want to run a command in 1 minute, all you need is to run the `at now +1 min` command. Then, when you get the at prompt, you write the command, as follows:

```
at> your_command
```

After this, press *Enter*. You will get the at prompt again. You can enter another command or number of commands that you want, with each one on a line. Then, type enter. Finally, run the *Ctrl+d* shortcut to close the at prompt.

In the same manner, you can type `at now +7 days` to run a command after 7 days. Alternatively, if you would like to execute a command at a specific date, you can run `at` followed by the date in the `dd/mm/yy` format.

If you want to check the list (queue) of the at jobs that were set to run after you finish entering the commands, as discussed previously, you have to run the `atq` command. If you are a new user, you can see your own queued at jobs. Only the root user can see everyone's queued at jobs. The `atrm` command, followed by the job number (given at the creation step or via the `atq` command), is used to delete an at job from the queue.

The `at` command is used to queue up a command that is supposed to run only once. If you want to set up commands so that they run repeatedly, you can use the `cron` facility, which allows you to script the `cron` jobs scheduled in the `crontab` files. Generally, there is one system `crontab` file (which is `/etc/crontab`), but each user can create their personal `crontab` file that allows them to launch commands at the times that they choose. To create a personal `crontab` file, you need to type the following command:

```
crontab -e
```

The `crontab -e` command opens the `crontab` file in case it exists, or it creates a new one using a text editor from your choice:

```
abdelmonam@abdelmonam-tactic:~$ crontab -e
no crontab for abdelmonam - using an empty one

Select an editor.  To change later, run 'select-editor'.
  1. /bin/ed
  2. /bin/nano            <---- easiest
  3. /usr/bin/emacs23
  4. /usr/bin/vim.tiny

Choose 1-4 [2]:
```

In a `crontab` file, each job is represented by a single line that determines when to run the job, followed by the command that needs to be run. For the `times` fields, they are in the following order: **minute (m)**, **hour (h)**, **day of month (dom)**, **month (mon)**, and **day of the week (dow)**. You can use * in these fields (for `any`).

> The following are the fields from left to right: minute (0 to 59), hour (0 to 23), date of the month (0 to 31), month (0 to 12 or Jan, Feb, Mar, Apr, May, Jun, Jul, Aug, Sep, Oct, Nov, or Dec), and day of the week (0 to 7 or Sun, Mon, Tue, Wed, Thu, Fri, or Sat). An asterisk (*) in a field means that any value for that field can be matched.

You can use a single value for each field or more than one. For example, for the `dow` field, you can use the **Mon, Fri** value to run a job at every beginning and end of the week (every **Monday** and **Friday**). Providing another example, for the `mon` field, a value of 1,4,7,10 means that the job will be launched in the first month of each quarter (January, April, July, and October).

The output of the `crontab` jobs (including errors) is sent via an e-mail to the user belongs to the `crontab` file (unless redirected).

To list the contents of your `crontab` file, you should run `crontab -l`, and to delete your `crontab` file, you should run `crontab -r`.

Summary

In this chapter, we saw different aspects of configuring and administering the Ubuntu Server system. We were introduced to CLI using network settings, package management, and administration tasks.

In the next chapter, we will start a new part of this book, which involves service creation and management.

3
Deploying Servers on Ubuntu

Hundreds of different services can be deployed on an Ubuntu Server, and each one of these services can be detailed in an entire book. In this chapter, we will have a look at the essentials of setting up and configuring some of the most common servers that system administrators need. Newbies will get a step-by-step guide, and advanced users will discover the Ubuntu approach towards servers. We will start with the deployment of the famous OpenSSH server. Then, we'll move on to set up a DNS server. After that, we will cover how to turn on a web and an e-mail server. Finally, we will cover how to deploy a database, DHCP, and file server.

The following topics are covered in the chapter:

- Deploying an OpenSSH server
- Setting up a DNS server
- Turning on a web server
- Deploying a mail server
- Setting up a database server
- Setting up a DHCP server
- Installing a file server

Deploying an OpenSSH server

Let's start with the most useful server that, according to me, every administrator should install on their server, irrespective of the aim of this server and the services that need to be put on it. It is the **OpenSSH** server that allows you to remotely connect in a secure way to a server from a computer that can reach this server. The OpenSSH server is a set of tools that allow, besides the secure remote connection, a secure file transfer with the help of the scp protocol.

The OpenSSH server allows clients to connect using many authentication methods, such as a plain password, a public key, and kerberos tickets.

Installing the OpenSSH server

We can install only the OpenSSH server, but in general, we need both the OpenSSH tools—a server and a client. We need a server to connect to the Ubuntu Server that we are working on from a reachable computer. We require a client to connect it to another server or computer.

Installing OpenSSH (the server and client) is quite easy. To install the OpenSSH client, you need to run the following command:

```
sudo apt-get install openssh-client
```

For the OpenSSH server, we previously saw that we can install it by using the `tasksel` utility during the Ubuntu Server installation process, but if you forgot to do this in the preceding step, you need to run the following command:

```
sudo apt-get install openssh-server
```

To install both the client and the server at once, you can simply run the following command:

```
sudo apt-get install ssh
```

Configuring the OpenSSH server

The OpenSSH server is handled by the `sshd` daemon. Its configuration is located in the `/etc/ssh/sshd_config` file, which can be modified by editing it.

A bad manipulation of this file can alter the SSH server work and break it. Therefore, it is better to start by performing a backup for this file and, as a security measurement, set the backup file as read-only by using the following commands:

```
sudo cp /etc/ssh/sshd_config
/etc/ssh/sshd_config.original
```

```
sudo chmod a-w /etc/ssh/sshd_config.original
```

Let's have a look at a couple of examples of what you can change by using this file. For the first example, find the port number. By default, sshd is listening on port 22. You can change this behavior and configure it to make it listen on port 2233 by setting the value of the port directive to 2233 inside this file. You will also find the **HostKey** directive, which allows us to set authentication keys paths. Another example is an instance where you would like to show the banner message that exists in the /etc/issue.net file as a pre-login message by commenting out the following line:

```
#Banner /etc/issue.net
```

If you would like to know more about the configuration directives that can be changed, and the eventual values and their use, just run the man sshd_config command.

After making modifications in the /etc/ssh/sshd_config file, you should save it and then restart the daemon by using the sudo service ssh restart command.

> Be careful when editing this file from a remote location, especially when the remote connection is the only way of reaching the server, because modifying this file can change the way it behaves when interacting with the network. Besides, in case there are some errors in this file and you restart the sshd daemon, the server may not start again and you will lose the connection on the server. Therefore, be careful and prepare your plan B (for example, having someone on site to reestablish the connection by restoring the original backup file).
>
> Note that by running /usr/bin/sshd -t, you can test the config file before restarting the server and thus avoid the eventual problems that we talked about in the preceding section.

Setting up a DNS server

A **DNS** is a **domain name system** server that answers queries about domain names by providing the relative IP address. It is a must for www working; without it, users will have to learn the IP addresses of every website that they want to visit and type them manually in their browser (or add them manually to host files), which is impossible.

There are a lot of programs that provide DNS services under Ubuntu, but the most common one is BIND.

The BIND installation

If you missed installing BIND during the Ubuntu Server installation, you can do it now, and there is more than one way of doing that.

You can either use the `tasksel` utility, which will automatically install for you the two `bind9` and `bind9-doc` packages. Alternatively, you can use the `apt-get` tool, as follows:

```
sudo apt-get install bind9 bind9-doc
```

Once the BIND packages are installed, it is fully configured and functional with the default parameters that allow it to work as a caching DNS for recursive queries. You can of course customize it to fit your needs. We will discuss how to do that in the following sections.

You can check BIND's status by using the following command:

```
sudo service bind9 status
```

In case it is not running, you can launch it by using the following command:

```
sudo service bind9 start
```

The output of this command is shown in the following screenshot:

```
abdelmonam@abdelmonam: ~
File  Edit  View  Search  Terminal  Help
abdelmonam@abdelmonam:~$ sudo service bind9 status
● bind9.service - BIND Domain Name Server
     Loaded: loaded (/lib/systemd/system/bind9.service; enabled; vendor preset: en
abled)
  Drop-In: /run/systemd/generator/bind9.service.d
           └─50-insserv.conf-$named.conf
   Active: active (running) since Sat 2015-07-11 01:07:34 UTC; 6s ago
     Docs: man:named(8)
 Main PID: 2564 (named)
   CGroup: /system.slice/bind9.service
           └─2564 /usr/sbin/named -f -u bind

Jul 11 01:07:35 abdelmonam named[2564]: automatic empty zone: 8.B.D.0.1.0.0....A
Jul 11 01:07:35 abdelmonam named[2564]: command channel listening on 127.0.0...3
Jul 11 01:07:35 abdelmonam named[2564]: command channel listening on ::1#953
Jul 11 01:07:35 abdelmonam named[2564]: managed-keys-zone: loaded serial 0
Jul 11 01:07:35 abdelmonam named[2564]: zone 0.in-addr.arpa/IN: loaded serial 1
Jul 11 01:07:35 abdelmonam named[2564]: zone 127.in-addr.arpa/IN: loaded ser...1
Jul 11 01:07:35 abdelmonam named[2564]: zone localhost/IN: loaded serial 2
Jul 11 01:07:35 abdelmonam named[2564]: zone 255.in-addr.arpa/IN: loaded ser...1
Jul 11 01:07:35 abdelmonam named[2564]: all zones loaded
Jul 11 01:07:35 abdelmonam named[2564]: running
Hint: Some lines were ellipsized, use -l to show in full.
abdelmonam@abdelmonam:~$
```

Ubuntu's BIND conventions

BIND files may have an organization in Ubuntu that is different from the ones in other distributions. The following are the basic files and directories:

- `/etc/bind`: This is the main directory for the BIND configuration files. It also contains the `zone` files.

- `/etc/bind/named.conf`: This is BIND's main configuration file. It includes scripts from other files, with the most notable ones being: `/etc/bind/named.conf.default-zones`, which contains a default zone such as local host; `/etc/bind/named.conf.local`, which contains zones added by the system administrator (use this file when you would like to add zones); and `/etc/bind/named.conf.options`, which contains additional options such as forwarders' addresses.

- `/etc/bind/db.*`: The zone files, which contain information related to each zone, have the convention of starting with `db.`, and each file identifies a particular zone.

- `/etc/init.d/bind9`: This is the file that contains the BIND startup parameters that are needed to launch the service.

- `/var/log/syslog`: By default, BIND uses this file to store its logs. This file contains the log of a lot of other services. So, if you would like to have only the BIND log, you can simply search for the named keyword using the `grep` command, as follows:

```
grep named /var/log/syslog
```

Configuring BIND

Configuring BIND is simple. It is always about creating new zones (or editing the existing ones). This is done by performing the following three steps:

1. Either create a zone file relative to the zone that needs to be added, or edit an existing one.

2. Add a reference to the zone file in `/etc/bind/named.conf.local`

3. Reload the BIND service by using the following command:

```
sudo service bind9 reload
```

Zone file configuration

The details related to a specific domain name are stored in a DNS server in an entity called **zone**. Each zone is represented by a file under the `/etc/bind/` directory. In this section, we will take a look at how to configure a DNS zone file.

If you would like to get more information about this subject, a complete tutorial on zone files and their contents is available at http://www.slashroot.in/what-dns-zone-file-complete-tutorial-zone-file-and-its-contents.

The zone files have the same structure. So, an easy way of configuring a new zone is by copying an existing zone file (such as /etc/bind/db.local) and then modifying it as required.

By default, timers in the zone file are set in seconds. You can use other time units such as the day by adding the letter d to the value, the week by adding the letter w, the hour using the letter h, and so on.

The following are the most important fields in the zone file configuration:

- **SOA: Start of Authority**, this server is considered to be the best source of information
- **NS**: This is the name servers for the zone file
- **A**: This is IPv4 address
- **AAAA**: This is IPv6 address
- **MX**: This is the mail server

You also need to configure a reversed DNS file for every zone that you create. The structure is also the same, so you can just copy one of the default reversed zones, such as /etc/bind/db.127.

To reference a zone file inside /etc/bind/named.conf.local, you need to just copy a sample of an existing reference and modify it. The following is an example that demonstrates this:

```
zone "localhost" {
  type master;
  file "/etc/bind/db.local";
};
zone "127.in-addr.arpa" {
  type master;
  file "/etc/bind/db.127";
};
```

When you reload BIND, it will take into consideration the modified zone file that has a higher serial number. So, be sure to increment the serial field in the zone file each time you modify it. If you don't do this, your modifications will be ignored. Most system administrators use the yyyyMMddHHmm format for this field.

DNS redundancy

DNS is a critical service for web and e-mail applications. So, it is important to have a redundancy of the main DNS server (called **salve**), which has the same information as the **master** DNS server.

To configure this, you have to add the salve server to the zone file in the master server by using the NS record. Then, when referencing the zone file, you should add the allow-transfer option to the zone definition inside the master DNS to allow the slave DNS to copy the data from it. You can also add the also-notify option so that the master DNS will notify the slave DNS for every modification inside that zone. On the other hand, in the slave server, the zone definition should contain the slave type and point to the master server. As an example, if we assume that the IP address of the master DNS is *192.168.1.1* and the IP address of the slave DNS is *192.168.1.2*, we should get the following output:

On the `master` server you will find the following output:

```
zone "localhost" {
  type master;
  file "/etc/bind/db.local";
  allow-transfer { 192.168.1.2; };
  also-notify { 192.168.1.2; };
};
zone "127.in-addr.arpa" {
  type master;
  file "/etc/bind/db.127";
  allow-transfer { 192.168.1.2; };
  also-notify { 192.168.1.2; };
};
```

On the `slave` server you will find the following output:

```
zone "localhost" {
  type slave;
  file "/etc/bind/db.local";
  masters { 192.168.1.1; };
};
```

```
zone "127.in-addr.arpa" {
  type slave;
  file "/etc/bind/db.127";
  masters { 192.168.1.1; };
};
```

DNS testing

To test whether your DNS is working, you should request to server and check the correctness of the information. To do this, you should either use a computer in which you point your name server to this DNS, or simply add the IP address of that DNS server as a parameter.

The famous NsLookup tool is the simplest tool to test DNS and reverse DNS. There is also the `dig` utility, which gives a richer answer, and the host tool, which is similar to NsLookup.

Turning on a web server

There are a lot of open source web servers that we can deploy on the Ubuntu Server, such as Apache Tomcat, NGINX, and Jetty. Each web server should be installed and configured to deal with a specific programming language. We should also install its libraries, along with the installation and configuration of the database that is necessary for the web server. Instead of doing all of this, especially when you need a web server to deploy an application developed in PHP, Perl, or Python, the best choice is to install a LAMP server.

LAMP is the abbreviation for **Linux Apache MySQL PHP** (or sometimes **Perl** or **Python**). It is the de facto standard for a web server deployment based on a combination of the Apache web server program that is used with Perl, PHP, or Python for dynamic content handling, and a MySQL database on the backend, with all of these components running on a Linux server. It has become a common way of setting up a web server deployment under Linux. That's the reason why Ubuntu has grouped all the necessary packages together—to simplify using LAMP inside an Ubuntu Server.

The LAMP Installation

There are a few different ways of setting up a web server on a default Ubuntu Server installation. Probably the easiest method is selecting the LAMP server during the initial installation, or afterwards with the `tasksel` tool. This will add the `apache2`, `apache2-mpm-prefork`, `mysql-server-5.6`, `mysql-client-5.6`, and `php5-mysql` packages along with all of their libraries and other dependencies. Alternatively, you can install each of these packages from the command line using the `apt-get install` tool.

During installation, the package manager will ask you to enter the root password of the MySQL database, as shown in the following screenshot:

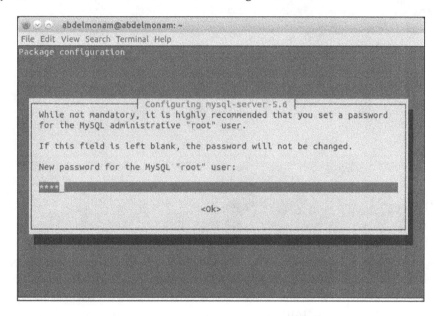

Entering the password is optional. You can keep it empty, but for security reasons it is recommended that you set a root password for the MySQL database. If you don't do that, anyone with an account on the server can access your database and read, alter, and even delete data.

After installing the LAMP server, there is an additional program that is very helpful and which can be installed. This program is called **phpMyAdmin**. It is a LAMP application that was specifically written for the administration of MySQL servers. It provides an easy graphical interface for database administration tasks that are written in PHP and which can be accessed via a web browser.

To install it, run the following command:

```
sudo apt-get install phpmyadmin
```

During installation, you will be asked to choose the web server that you want to configure for phpMyAdmin. In our case, it is apache2, as shown in the following screenshot:

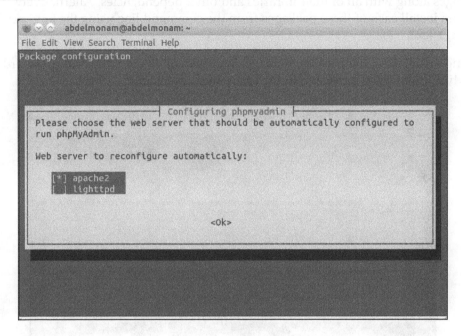

You can test the LAMP server by using the IP address of the Ubuntu Server on your web browser. You should get the Apache2 default page. Also, you can test phpmyadmin by using <ubuntu-server-IP>/phpmyadmin. You will get the login interface (use the MySQL parameters to log in to phpmyadmin).

Ubuntu's LAMP Conventions

Like most other distributions, Ubuntu has certain conventions when it comes to the Apache administration. Configuration files are organized in a particular way, as are administrative tools and logs. If you aren't used to the way Debian and Ubuntu organize Apache, it is quite different from what you may have seen on other distributions. Here are the major file conventions for Apache:

- `/etc/apache2`: This directory contains all the Apache configuration files. Formerly, Apache was configured via one large `httpd.conf` file, which contained options, settings, and different virtual hosts. Actually, this file is empty because Ubuntu has moved away from the monolithic `httpd.conf` model and has split up its configuration across a number of files and subdirectories.

- `/etc/apache2/apache2.conf`: This is the main Apache configuration file that is used by Ubuntu's Apache2 binary. The default `apache2.conf` file is heavily commented. So, it works well as a guide in and of itself to each configuration option and what it does.

- `/etc/apache2/envvars`: This file contains the definition of the environment variables used by different scripts when Apache starts to define settings such as the location of the PID files.

- `/etc/apache2/ports.conf`: This file is used to define which ports Apache listens on when it starts. The default settings make it listen on the standard port *80,* and additionally on port *443* when the SSL module is enabled.

- `/etc/apache2/conf.d/`: This directory is listed as an included directory in the main `apache2.conf` file, which means that when Apache starts, it will also include the configuration files found in this directory and add them to the overall configuration. This directory is used for additional Apache options that an administrator (or a package) might want to add separately from the core `apache2.conf` file.

- `/etc/apache2/mods-available/`: Ubuntu offers a simpler and more modular approach than the traditional way of adding modules. All the modules that are available on the system are represented within this directory by the .load and `.conf` files.

- `/etc/apache2/mods-enabled/`: This directory basically contains symbolic links to the .load and .conf files in the `mods-enabled` directory. When Apache starts, it will scan this directory and load all the modules referenced within the directory. So for instance, if you want to enable the SSL module, you can run `sudo ln -s /etc/apache2/mod-available/ssl.load /etc/apache2/mods-enabled/ssl.load`. Ubuntu even provides tools to simplify this. To enable a module, just run `a2enmod`, followed by the module that you want to enable. For example, to enable the SSL module as we did previously, just run `sudo a2enmod ssl`. Likewise, there is an `a2dismod` program that will disable a module for you. It takes the same syntax as `a2enmod`. So, to disable SSL, execute `sudo a2dismod ssl`.

- `/etc/apache2/sites-available/`: Ubuntu organizes the Apache virtual hosts in a similar way to how it organizes modules. Under Ubuntu, every virtual host or site that is available to be served by Apache on this machine has its configuration in a separate file under sites-available.

- `/etc/apache2/sites-enabled/`: Like `mods-enabled`, this directory contains symbolic links to configuration files in sites-available. So, when you want to add a new virtual host to Apache, just create a new configuration file for the host that contains a complete `<VirtualHost>` block under sites-available, and **symbolic link (symlink)** it here:

```
sudo ln -s /etc/apache2/sites-available/mysite
/etc/apache2/sites-enabled/mysite
```

  Alternatively, you can use the `a2ensite` script that works just like `a2enmod`. Just run `a2enmod` with the site that you wish to enable as an argument. To enable `mysite`, type `sudo a2ensite mysite`, and to disable it you can use `a2dissite`, as follows:

```
sudo a2dissite mysite
```

- `/var/www/`: This is the default document root for Apache. An HTML file that is readable by Apache and placed in this directory will be available once you point a web browser at the server. There is already a default `index.html` in this directory.

- `/usr/lib/cgi-bin/`: This is the default location for the CGI scripts. The scripts referenced on the web server by `/cgi-bin` will point here.

- `/var/log/apache2/`: This is the standard directory in which the Apache logs are stored. The `access.log` file contains information about the files that have been accessed on the web server, and the `error.log` file lists the Apache errors. In case you have trouble starting Apache, look in `error.log` for clues.

 To activate the new configuration, you need to run the following command:
`sudo service apache2 restart`

Apache management and testing

In the following section, we will discover one of the most helpful Apache tools named `apache2ctl`, and some of its applications.

apache2ctl

The `/usr/sbin/apache2ctl` program is the primary command-line program that you will use to manage Apache under Ubuntu. The syntax for the command is fairly straightforward. Run `apache2ctl` from the command line and pass a single command to it as an argument. The simple start, stop, and restart commands will, as you might imagine, start, stop, and restart the Apache process respectively. You can also achieve the same functionality with the `apache2 init` script. Therefore, the three commands that do the same thing are as follows:

```
sudo apache2ctl restart
sudo /etc/init.d/apache2 restart
sudo service apache2 restart
```

Stopping Apache gracefully

There is a potential risk associated with the `restart` and `stop` commands. When you restart or stop Apache with these commands, all the currently running Apache processes are killed, even if they are in the middle of serving files to a user. If you issue a `restart` command when a user is in the middle of loading a page, it will only load as much information as it currently has and then stop loading a page, thus forcing users to reload the page. To avoid this, `apache2ctl` has provided the `graceful` and `graceful-stop` commands.

These commands restart and stop Apache respectively, but when they do, they wait for each process to finish the outstanding requests first. On an active site, a graceful restart won't even be noticed by anyone using the service. In general, unless you know that a site is not actively serving traffic (or unless you don't care whether all the active connections are closed), you should use `graceful` and `graceful-stop`. The only exception is when you add new SSL certificates to a site or make other changes that do require a full Apache restart to take effect.

Diagnostic apache2ctl commands

The other main commands for `apache2ctl` provide more diagnostic features. The first, `configtest`, will test the current Apache configuration files for errors. This can be very useful in case you decide to automate the deployment of Apache scripts. When you set up a script to deploy configuration files and restart Apache, a challenge that you may face is that in case you have made a mistake in the configuration files, Apache might not start a back up. If you deploy the same file to the entire web farm, you may potentially bring the entire web farm down with a single syntax error and a script that blindly deploys and restarts Apache. With `configtest`, you can set up logic in your deployment scripts that restarts Apache once a server has passed the `configtest` command.

As an Apache server gets traffic, you typically want to get diagnostic information from it, such as how many Apache processes are active, what those processes are doing, and how many open slots you still have available. The status and fullstatus apache2ctl commands provide you with a lot of great diagnostic data. The status command outputs a general-purpose overall status of the Apache server, including how long the server has been up, how many requests are active, and how many processes are idle. In addition to this, it outputs an ASCII art map of all the available processes with different letters representing different process states. The fullstatus command outputs similar information, with just more of it and in more detail.

Deploying an e-mail server

Along with the Web, e-mail is probably the service that most people think of when they think of the Internet. Like web servers, e-mail servers have traditionally been pretty tricky to set up, and there are many guides and books on this subject. However, you will find that e-mail servers are pretty easy to set up and use under Ubuntu.

Installing an e-mail server requires you to manage the sending and receiving of e-mails. These two notions are important because they implement two different protocols—**SMTP** to send, and **POP** or **IMAP** to receive the messages.

When a user sends an e-mail it is in fact never in direct contact with the recipient. The e-mail goes through at least two servers that are, in order, the sending server (SMTP), called the **MTA (Mail Transfer Agent)**, which sends it to the receiver server (POP or IMAP), called **MDA (Mail Delivery Agent)**, possibly transiting the e-mail via other SMTP servers as well. Then, the e-mail will wait on this last server until the recipient launches its e-mail client (such as Thunderbird), which will retrieve the message from the receiving server via one of the two POP or IMAP protocols.

We can find all of these servers located on the same machine or different machines; it depends on the dimension of the e-mail server that you want to use.

Also note that to have a working e-mail server that sends and receives mails to and from the Internet, you should have a working DNS server with a valid domain name that you own.

If you would like to avoid assembling the different pieces of an e-mail server, and at the same time use a very powerful mailing server on Ubuntu, you can opt for a solution such as the famous Zimbra server. Explaining how to install and administrate Zimbra needs more than a section in a chapter. That's why I wrote a book about it named *Learning Zimbra Server Essentials*, Packt Publishing, in October 2013 (for more information, visit https://www.packtpub.com/networking-and-servers/learning-zimbra-server-essentials). If you want, you can refer to it.

Now, let's discover how to handle every piece of the e-mail server.

The MTA server

There are a lot of **Mail Transfer Agent** (**MTAs**) that can be deployed on an Ubuntu Server, but the most famous MTA one is **Postfix**, because it is a good, secure, and an easy-to-administer e-mail server. Besides, it is the default e-mail server that Ubuntu uses when you select **Mail server** in `tasksel`.

Installing Postfix

Postfix can be installed with the same methods that are used by many of the other services that I mentioned in this chapter. You can choose **Mail server** either during the initial installation or when you run the `tasksel` program. Alternatively, you can use the following command:

```
sudo apt-get install postfix
```

When you install Postfix, the installer will launch the initial Postfix configuration script. It is an interactive program that provides you with a few standard common e-mail server configurations. Based on your choice, it will propose a few more options so that at the end of this process, you should at least have a functional e-mail server.

First of all, it gives you an overview of the different configuration modes that you can adopt, as shown in the following screenshot:

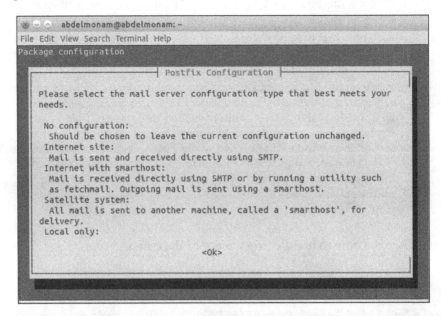

Then, it will give you the options to choose. In our case, we will choose **Internet site**, as shown in the following screenshot, so that we can directly send and receive e-mails using SMTP:

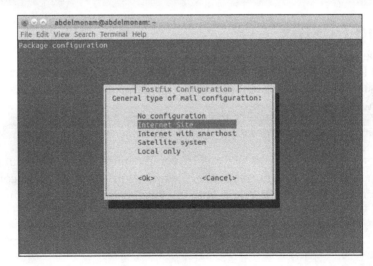

Finally, it asks you about the domain name that you will use for this e-mail server. This is the domain name that you will use to send e-mails. In our case, we will choose `ubuntu-essentials.net`, which will allow us to send mail such as `contact@ ubuntu-essentials.net`, as shown in the following screenshot:

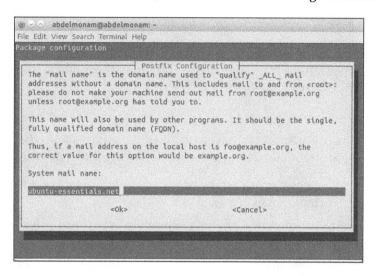

Keep in mind that although the e-mail server will function, you will need to perform some extra configurations if you want to add greylisting, spam/virus checking, IMAP or POP servers, or other advanced options.

During the installation process, you will be asked for only a few details. Therefore, to complete the customization of the other necessary parameters, such as the trusted subnets, the default mailbox size, and the root address, you can run the following command after finishing the installation process and follow the given steps:

```
sudo dpkg-reconfigure postfix
```

Managing Postfix

There aren't too many surprises with Ubuntu's Postfix conventions. Most of the directories and files used by Postfix under Ubuntu follow the same structure on other platforms. For example, the `/etc/postfix/` directory contains a majority of the Postfix configuration files, especially `/etc/postfix/main.cf`, where you can activate secure authentication using SSL, install TLS certificates for signature and encryption, and make use of a lot of other options. The `/var/spool/mail/` directory contains the users' mailboxes, and `/var/log/mail.*` are the log files.

The main tool that you will use to administer Postfix is aptly named postfix. It works much like `apache2ctl` in that it accepts a few different commands as arguments and can also be used as a substitute for the `init` script to start and stop the service. For instance, to stop Postfix and then start it again, type in the following command:

```
sudo postfix stop
sudo postfix start
```

For other parameters and their explanation, you can get them from the `man` command via the following command:

```
man postfix
```

In addition to the Postfix command-line tool, Postfix provides a few other tools to help you with the administration of the services. The following are some of these tools:

- The `postqueue` command can be used by regular users to get information about the current e-mail queue.

- The `postsuper` command allows a superuser to perform privileged operations on a queue.

- The `postconf` command outputs every Postfix setting to the screen along with its value. This can be very useful in case you modify the main `config` file and you would like to get the active running configuration before reloading. So for example, if you want to see the current value of `myhostname` in the running `config` file, we just have to type the following command:

```
sudo postconf | grep ^myhostname
```

The MDA server

Like for MTA, there is a lot of MDA software that exist under the official Ubuntu repositories and which differs in terms of complexity and functionalities besides the interoperability with other e-mail server components, such as Postfix. For this example, I will cover the Dovecot POP and IMAP servers, as they integrate well with Postfix, support Maildirs, and have a number of additional packages available that provide advanced features such as LDAP, MySQL, and Postgres support. The steps are pretty simple. They start with enabling Maildirs on Postfix and then installing Dovecot.

Maildir is a specific directory structure that is used to save e-mails instead of the traditional manner of using the `mbox` format. It should be enabled on Postfix by setting the `home_mailbox` variable inside the `/etc/postfix/main.cf` file, as follows:

```
home_mailbox = Maildir/
```

Alternatively, to enable it, you can just run the following command:

```
sudo postconf -e 'home_mailbox = Maildir/'
```

You should of course reload `postfix` after this step by using the following command:

```
sudo postfix reload
```

Then, move on to install Dovecot by using the following command:

```
sudo apt-get install dovecot-imapd dovecot-pop3d
```

This will install and enable POP, POP with SSL, IMAP, and IMAP with SSL.

After this, you can customize Dovecot by using the main `/etc/dovecot/dovecot.conf` config file. Don't forget to reload the daemon every time you modify the `config` file using the `sudo /etc/init.d/dovecot reload` command to implement the changes.

The next step is to tell Dovecot to use Maildirs and also let it know where it can find them on the system. To do this, check whether there is already an uncommented line that starts with `mail_location` (in the default installation, it's commented out). If it doesn't exist, then add the following line; if it does exist, then modify the `mail_location` line so that it looks like the following line:

```
mail_location = maildir:~/Maildir
```

Then, reload Dovecot by using the `sudo /etc/init.d/dovecot reload` command. Now, you should be able to configure e-mail clients to point to the server and access their local e-mail.

Filters and security for an e-mail server

Today, **Unsolicited Bulk Email (UBE)** represents one of the largest problems for e-mail servers. Also known as **spam**, such messages may also carry viruses and other forms of malware. To handle this issue, there are a lot of powerful utilities that can be installed on an Ubuntu Server and integrated with an e-mail server. The following is a list of the best utilities:

- **Amavisd-new** is a generic scanner program. Its role is to call a certain number of content filtering tools such as antivirus, spam detection, and so on. You can install it by using the following command:

  ```
  sudo apt-get install amavisd-new.
  ```

To configure it, you have to first of all activate antivirus and anti-spam detection in Amavisd-new by editing the `/etc/amavis/conf.d/15-content_filter_mode` file and uncommenting some lines, as described in the file itself. To customize Amavisd-new, you can edit options in the `config` files under the `/etc/amavis/conf.d/` directory. Don't forget to restart the daemon by using the following command:

```
sudo service amavis restart
```

For integration with Postfix, you have to enter the following command:

```
sudo postconf -e 'content_filter =
smtp-amavis:[127.0.0.1]:10024'
```

Then, edit `/etc/postfix/master.cf` by adding the following to the end of the file:

```
smtp-amavis     unix    smtp
-o smtp_data_done_timeout=1200
-o smtp_send_xforward_command=yes
-o disable_dns_lookups=yes
-o max_use=20
127.0.0.1:10025 inet    n   smtpd
-o content_filter=
-o local_recipient_maps=
-o relay_recipient_maps=
-o smtpd_restriction_classes=
-o smtpd_delay_reject=no
-o smtpd_client_restrictions=permit_mynetworks,reject
-o smtpd_helo_restrictions=
-o smtpd_sender_restrictions=
-o smtpd_recipient_restrictions=permit_mynetworks,reject
-o smtpd_data_restrictions=reject_unauth_pipelining
-o smtpd_end_of_data_restrictions=
-o mynetworks=127.0.0.0/8
-o smtpd_error_sleep_time=0
-o smtpd_soft_error_limit=1001
-o smtpd_hard_error_limit=1000
-o smtpd_client_connection_count_limit=0
-o smtpd_client_connection_rate_limit=0
-o receive_override_options=
no_header_body_checks,no_unknown_recipient_checks,
no_milters
```

To prevent messages that are generated to report spam from being classified as spam, add the following two lines immediately below the pickup transport service:

```
-o content_filter=
-o receive_override_options=no_header_body_checks
```

Finally, restart Postfix by using the following command:

```
sudo service postfix restart
```

At this step, content filtering with spam and virus detection is enabled.

- **Spamassassin** is the most used open source anti-spam program in the world today. It uses a variety of mechanisms to filter e-mails based on message content. You can install it via the `sudo apt-get install spamassassin` command. To activate the `spamassassin` daemon, you have to change the value of the enabled parameter from *0* to *1* in the `/etc/default/spamassassin` file. Then, start the daemon by using the following command:

```
sudo service spamassassin start
```

- **ClamAV** is the most known open source antivirus application. You can install it by using the `sudo apt-get install clamav-daemon` command. The default configuration of ClamAV fits our needs. Therefore, we can start working with it. However, you can customize it by using the `config` files in `/etc/clamav`.

> You need to add the ClamAV and Amavis users to each other's groups in order for Amavisd-new to have appropriate access to scan files and prevent ownership issues from inhibiting scans, as follows:
>
> ```
> sudo adduser clamav amavis
> sudo adduser amavis clamav
> ```

- **Postgrey** is a program that implements greylisting for the Postfix server. **Greylisting** is a technique that helps you cut down on the amount of spam a server receives. You can install it by using the `sudo apt-get install postgrey` command. For its configuration, all that you have to do is modify the `smtpd_recipient_restrictions` option in Postfix's `main.cf` file to add the `localhost:10023` service.

- The **OpenDKIM** implements a **Sendmail Mail Filter** (**Milter**) for the **DomainKeys Identified Mail** (**DKIM**) standard, and `python-postfix-policyd-spf` enables **Sender Policy Framework** (**SPF**) to check it with Postfix. You can install OpenDKIM via the following command:

```
sudo apt-get install opendkim postfix-policyd-spf-python
```

To get more knowledge about this subject, visit `https://mandrill.`
`zendesk.com/hc/en-us/articles/205582267-What-are-SPF-and-DKIM-`
`and-how-do-I-set-them-up-.`

- The **Spamassassin** process can be enhanced by using some optional packages that integrate with it, for better spam detection. We can install these packages by using the `sudo apt-get install pyzor razor` command. Spamassassin automatically detects optional components and will use these components if they are present. So, there is no need to configure `pyzor` and `razor`.

- To filter e-mail attachments, we need the main filtering application's compression utilities, which can be installed by using the following command:

```
sudo apt-get install arj cabextract cpio lha nomarch pax
rar unrar unzip zip
```

Other facilities

After installing an e-mail server, you can use it by configuring an e-mail client such as Thunderbird or Evolution. You can also access it via the Web if you have already installed a webmail client. There are a lot of webmail clients that you can install. All that you need is a working MTA and MDA, along with a web server. We have covered these topics in the previous sections. Then, you should install the webmail solution and configure it to work with your e-mail server. You can choose a solution from SquirrelMail, Horde, OpenWebMail, and Roundcube. As an example, we will install and configure Roundcube. To do this, you need to run the `sudo apt-get` `install roundcube-mysql roundcube` command. Then, edit the `/etc/roundcube/` `apache.conf` file and uncomment the following two lines:

```
Alias /roundcube/program/js/tiny_mce/ /usr/share/tinymce/www/
Alias /roundcube /var/lib/roundcube
```

Finally, restart Apache by using the following command:

```
sudo service apache2 restart
```

You can now access your webmail via `<domaine-name>/roundcube`. In our case, it is `www.buntu-essentials.net/roundcube`.

You can also install a mass mailing manager (a mailing list manager), such as the famous mailman, and configure it to work with the e-mail server in a manner that is similar to how you installed and configured the webmail client.

Setting up a database server

Databases are also one of most used services that every system administrator deals with every day. With the Ubuntu Server, installing and managing databases is quite simple. We previously saw how to install a MySQL database within a LAMP server. In this section, we will see how to do that as a separate action. We will also see how to install and manage another commonly used Open Source database server named Postgres.

The MySQL server

It is easy to install the MySQL database on Ubuntu, just run the following command:

```
sudo apt-get install mysql-server
```

You will be asked to enter the root password. You can leave it empty, but I recommend that you set one, and a good one (a strong password) is better.

For customization tasks, you can find the MySQL main configuration files under /etc/mysql/.

Ubuntu includes the `mysqladmin` tool to help you with MySQL administration. You can think of it as the `apache2ctl` program in that it accepts certain commands on the command line and then interacts with the `mysqld` process for you. For instance, to get the current status of your MySQL process, run the following command:

```
sudo mysqladmin -p status
```

> I used the -p argument in this command, which will tell `mysqladmin` to prompt me for the password on the command line. If you set a password for the root user, you will need to use -p with your commands. However, if you plan to run a batch of commands and don't want to enter the password every time, you can add the password to the -p option. So for instance, if the MySQL password was myP@ssword, type the following command:
>
> ```
> sudo mysqladmin -p myP@ssword status
> ```

The `mysqladmin` manual page (type man mysqladmin on a console) lists the full set of commands.

> The easiest way to manage a MySQL database is by using the phpMyAdmin utility. Have a look at how to install and configure it in the section named *Web Server* in this chapter.

The Postgre server

Even though MySQL has the reputation of being easy to use, PostgreSQL under Ubuntu is also simple to install and use. To install PostgreSQL, you can either select **PostgreSQL Server** as you install Ubuntu or do so afterwards with `tasksel`, or use a package manager to install the `postgresql` package, as follows:

```
sudo apt-get install postgresql
```

Once the `postgresql` package has been installed, the database service will start in the background and you can then set up your superuser account and create a database. The initial administration will be performed by the `postgres` user. So first, use `sudo` to become that user by using the following command:

```
sudo -u postgres -s
```

Now, from this shell, you can create a new user account by using the `createuser` program. On the other hand, the `dropuser` command deletes users. Creating databases is done via the `createdb` program, and accessing the database is done via the `psql` command.

As with MySQL, there is a PHP-based administration tool called **phpPgAdmin**. To install phpPgAdmin, you simply need to install the `phppgadmin` package, as follows:

```
sudo apt-get install phppgadmin
```

The package will download all of its dependencies, including a web server, in case one is not already installed. Once the package is installed, create a symlink to its Apache configuration file under `/etc/apache2/sites-available` and then use `a2ensite` to enable the site, as follows:

```
sudo ln -s /etc/phppgadmin/apache.conf /etc/apache2/sites-available/
phppgadmin
sudo a2ensite phppgadmin
sudo apache2ctl graceful
```

Setting up a DHCP server

DHCP stands for **Dynamic Host Control Protocol**. With this protocol, a new host on the network can issue a request for IP information. The DHCP server will then provide the host with all the necessary information that it needs to communicate on the network, such as its IP address, netmask, the gateway, and the DNS servers that need to be used.

Installing DHCP

Installing a DHCP server under Ubuntu is an easy task, just type the following command and you will get the DHCP server installed:

```
sudo apt-get install dhcp3-server
```

Ubuntu DHCP Conventions

It just needs additional configuration to be useful; we will see this in this section:

- `/etc/dhcp3/dhcpd.conf`: This is the configuration file for the DHCP server. By default, it is a heavily commented file that should provide plenty of examples for you to work on.

- `/var/lib/dhcp3/dhcpd.leases`: This file contains the current list of DHCP leases that your server has handed out. If you are wondering which MAC address got a particular IP or when a particular lease will expire, look in this file.

- `/var/log/syslog`: DHCP uses the standard `syslog` file for all of its logs. Here, you will be able to find requests from the network for a DHCP request along with the DHCP server's reply.

Configuring DHCP

Ubuntu provides a heavily commented DHCP configuration file that explains all the major options and gives a number of different configuration examples. For basic DHCP services, you generally want to set up one or possibly two scenarios—**dynamic DHCP** and **static DHCP**. In a dynamic DHCP configuration, new hosts get assigned an IP out of a possible range of IPs. There's no guarantee that a host will get assigned the same IP every time. With static DHCP, you can bind a particular IP address to a host's MAC address and ensure that every time it shows up on the network, it will get the same IP. Dynamic DHCP is good for a simple, easy-to-maintain DHCP server, and static DHCP gives you many benefits of static IPs without nearly as many headaches. Plus with static IPs, if you do want to change the IP address of a host, you can do so in the `dhcpd.conf` file and reload DHCP instead of having to track down and change the host.

Now, to reload DHCP and enable my settings, run the following command:

```
sudo service dhcp3-server restart
```

In case you didn't make a syntax error, the DHCP server will stop and then start again. If there is an error in the file, it should output an error to the screen along with its location. A common error is a missing semicolon at the end of a particular line.

Installing a file server

This is the last section in this chapter. In this section, we will discover how to install and configure, on an Ubuntu Server, two of the most used file servers – **FTP** and **Samba**.

The FTP server

The `vsftpd` is an FTP daemon available in Ubuntu. It is easy to install, set up, and maintain. To install `vsftpd`, run the following command:

```
sudo apt-get install vsftpd
```

The `/etc/vsftpd.conf` file contains the main configuration options for the FTP server. It is well commented. Therefore, you can edit it easily. After the `config` modification, you should restart the server by using the following command:

```
sudo restart vsftpd
```

Connecting to the FTP server is quite easy. You can do so either by using the FTP command in the CLI of the customer machine or a client GUI program such as FileZilla.

 With FTP, data is transmitted unencrypted over the network. To transmit data securely, you can either use the FTPS protocol (FTP over SSL), or advantageously turn to **SFTP** (**SSH File Transfer Protocol**).

The Samba server

Samba is a program that implements SMB and CIFS, the Windows file-sharing protocols. As such, it's ideal as a platform to share file under Windows, since all the clients can access the server without additional software. Over time, Samba has grown to support advanced sections of Windows file sharing to a point where it can operate like any other Windows file server or **Primary Domain Controller (PDC)**.

To install Samba, you can either select the **Samba Server** option during the Ubuntu installation or after the installation with the help of the `tasksel` program, or install the `samba`, `samba-doc`, `smbfs`, and `winbind` packages separately with the help of the package manager, as follows:

```
sudo apt-get install samba samba-doc smbfs winbind
```

The Samba service will start automatically. By default, of course nothing too interesting will be shared. So, you will need to tweak Samba's configuration files before any directories are shared. The main configuration files are located under the `/etc/samba/` directory, especially the core configuration file named `/etc/samba/smb.conf`. This file is heavily commented, and it contains a number of different examples of how to set up shares, including a useful example configuration.

After installing and configuring the Samba server, go to another host on the network and attempt to connect to the Samba server. On an Ubuntu desktop, navigate to **Places | Connect to Server**. Then, select **Windows share** from the **Service type** drop-down menu. Finally, enter the IP address or hostname of the Samba server and then enter the name that you put between the brackets in the `smb.conf` file for the name of the share. Click on **Connect**. Ubuntu will mount and display the mounted share on the desktop.

Summary

In this chapter, we went in depth in terms of deploying services on an Ubuntu Server. We discussed how to install and configure some of the most used servers that every system administrator will usually deal with.

In the next chapter, we will move on to the security aspect of an Ubuntu Server.

4
Security with Ubuntu

In the field of computer servers, security is a very hot key. That's why, Ubuntu Server gives it a lot of importance. In this chapter, we will take a look at how to activate, configure, and enhance a lot of security aspects. This chapter will be divided into the following three parts:

- Getting a basic security level for Ubuntu Server
- Going in depth to see how to configure advanced security settings
- Performing a backup/restore procedure for the whole Ubuntu Server

The basic security settings

First of all, let's have a look at how to set up a basic security level for Ubuntu Server. There is a saying in security circles that *security is a process, not a product*. What this means is that despite what your vendor might tell you, you can't solve all your security problems with some application or software. Instead, you will find real security when you start to follow good security principles and develop good security procedures. This is what we will mainly see in this section.

Managing users

In this subsection, you will discover best practices in terms of user management, which covers not only user creation, modification, and deletion, but also group attribution, permissions, and a lot of other details.

User account administration

The following are the most useful commands that are required to set up and manage user accounts:

- `useradd`: This command adds the user that was passed in as a parameter to the local authentication system
- `usermod`: This command modifies the properties of the user passed in as a parameter
- `userdel`: This command properly deletes from a system the user passed in as a parameter
- `passwd`: This command modifies the passwords for a user passed in as a parameter

We can add some options to those commands, those options are listed and detailed using -for example for the case of `useradd`- either `man useradd` or `useradd --help`.

> There exists the `adduser` command that also allows you to create new users. The difference between `useradd` and `adduser` depends on the Linux distribution. For example, for Fedora/Centos/Gentoo, `adduser` is just a symbolic link to `useradd`. But in our case, on Debian or Ubuntu systems, `useradd` is the command itself, and you can create users and define options for these users by using it. On the other hand, `adduser` is a Perl script that uses `useradd` to create an account and asks you for a password, your full name, phone number, and other information. We can say that in this case, it simplifies things for you.

The following are the most important options that you need to take into account when creating a new user, especially for security reasons:

- `-m`: Use this option during the creation of a home directory for the user that needs to be created. Without it, you'd have to create a new directory, change its ownership and permissions that fit the needs of the user, put within it the default files and directories that should exist under a home directory, and then assign the default directories and files to the home directory by using the `usermod` command with the `-d` option.
- `-e date`: This is used to set an expiration date for the user. After this date, the system will automatically disable the user's account. Use this in case you need to create temporary users for your server. So, even if you forget to delete them, the system will at least lock their accounts.

- -G groups: This sets the group membership of users. It is good security practice to classify server users by groups and set specific parameters and permissions for each group.

> Every user has a unique ID, which is the UID variable. In Ubuntu, this variable starts from *1,000* for regular users, and values under *500* are reserved for system accounts with a specification value; the UID variable *0* is reserved for root users. Normally, this UID is unique, but there is only one case where you may want to give the same UID to more than one user — when you want to create a backup root user. To do this, you need to use either the -o option, or the -u 0 option with the useradd command when creating a user.

Password administration

Passwords are one of the security keys for an **operating system (OS)**. In Ubuntu Server, passwords are managed by using the passwd command. A simple user can use it to change their password, and an administrator can use it to change the password of another regular user. Not only that, the passwd command has other important features, such as the following ones, which are useful in the maintenance of system security:

- By using the -l option, an administrator can lock a user account temporarily. It can be unlocked later by using the -u option.

- The status of the password for a given user account can be reported by using the -s option.

- Users can be forced to change their password during the next login by using the -e option.

- Setting a minimum number of days to use a password before the possibility of changing it again is done via the -n min_days_number option. This is useful when you wish to prevent users from changing their password after expiration and then changing it back to the old one immediately.

- You can set a maximum period of days to use a password. After completing this period, users are obliged to change their password. This is done by using the -x max_days_number option.

- You can notify a user about the expiration of their password; the period in days is specified in the argument of the -c notif option.

- You can also set an automatic expiration of a user account in case there is no activity for a given period. This period is set in days and passed as an argument of the -i exper option.

Some additional security features that are specifically related to password management and user login in general can be located and modified in the `/etc/login.defs` file. The following are the most important of these parameters:

- `FAIL_DELAY`: This sets the amount of time (in seconds) that is taken by a system after a failed login before a user is prompted again to re-enter their password. By default, it is 3 seconds. By setting a suitable value here, we can block a **brute force attack**.

- `LASTLOG_ENAB`: This is a Boolean value. When it is set to 1, it means that this feature is enabled. By enabling this feature, the system will log all the successful logins in the `/var/log/lastlog` file. The `lastlog` file should exist to have this feature working. In case it doesn't, you can create it by using the `touch /var/log/lastlog` command.

- `PASS_MIN_LEN`: This parameter contains the minimum number of characters that must be used for new passwords.

Permission settings

Permissions are the second security barrier after the login process in an OS. Ubuntu, like other Linux servers, has a strong and well-made permission structure. In this section, we will cover two main concepts—file ownership and operation permissions (read/write/execute).

File ownership

Each file on Ubuntu Server has its owner (user) and group owner (the user's primary group in general). In some cases, an administrator needs to change a file ownership for some reason (general security reasons). To do this, we have to call either the `chown` or `chgrp` command.

For `chown`, the command has the following pattern:

```
chown [OWNER][:[GROUP]] file
```

Here are a couple of examples of this command:

- `chown one_user some_file`: This command changes the owner of `some_file` to `one_user`.

- `chown one_user:one_group some_file`: This command not only does what the preceding command did, but also changes its group to `one_group`.

We can also use `chown` to change only the group ownership. An example of this is `chown .one_group some_file`. Don't forget the (.) character just before the group name, which is `one_group` in this case. Note that we recently started using the colon character (`:`); both `.` and `:` are doing the job.

For group ownership, there is another alternative, namely the `chgrp` command. An example of its usage is `chgrp one_group some_file`. Note that we don't need the `.` character before the group name, which is `one_group` in this case.

> By default, the scope of the `chown` and `chgrp` commands applies only to the file or directory on which they are used. If you want to use these commands in a recursive way, you just have to add the `-R` option. For example, `chown -R one_user some_dir` makes the `one_user` user the owner of all the files in `some_dir` and all of its subdirectories.

Configuring permissions

Operation permissions are of three types, namely **read** (the **r** symbol or a value of **4**), **write** (the **w** symbol or a value of **2**), and **execute** (the **x** symbol or a value of **1**). Each one of these three types can be applied on a file or directory for the **owner user (u)**, its **primary user group (g)** members, and **other users (o)**. We can apply permissions on **all users (a)**. To set these permissions, you can use the following two ways:

- **Specific use**: This is used to configure specific permissions for a specific file. This is done by using the `chmod` command.

- **General use**: This is used to configure default permissions attribution for new created files. This is done by using the `umask` command.

> There are some additional specific permissions called **special permissions**, namely **SUID**, **SGID**, and **Sticky bit**. This is beyond the scope of this book. You can explore them in an advanced Linux administration guide.

For the `chmod` tool, you can use the following two modes:

- The relative mode: This can be used in the same way as we use the absolute mode, which is detailed in the next section, to set huge changes at a time in terms of permissions, but it is even more useful when you need to add or remove just one permission at a time in an easy and convenient manner. When using `chmod` in this mode, you need to specify the entity (u, g, o, a) to which we will grant permissions, which is followed by the granting symbol (+ for adding, - for removing, and = for setting the permissions) and the permissions that you wish to apply (r, w, x). For example, the `chmod g+w some_file` command will add write permissions on the `some_file` file to the entity group. Let's take a look at another example where we set more than one permission at the same time by using the `chmod u+rwx,g+rx-w,o+r-wx another_file` mode, where we added all the rights to a user, added read and `execute` to the group and removed `write` from it, and added only `read` to others and removed `write` and `execute`.

- The absolute mode: This mode offers a short and convenient way to set permissions, especially when you need to change more than one permission at a time. In this mode, we use numeric values to define permissions. The permission value is composed of four digits. The first one refers to the special permissions (not covered in this book, as explained in a previous note). This digit can be omitted, unless you want to use it (be careful because it is dangerous). The other values refer in the order from left to right to the permissions related to a user, group, and others. Values are counted for each entity by adding values related to each permission (r=4, w=2, x=1). For example, the equivalent of `chmod u+rwx,g+rx-w,o+r-wx another_file` should be `chmod 754 another_file`.

For the `umask` tool, it is the **user file creation mode mask**. It determines the default permissions that are set when creating a new file. The `umask` parameter is expressed in a numeric value, and this value is subtracted from the maximum permissions that can be set automatically; which is *666* for files and *777* for directories. The order of digits used in `umask` is the same as that for `chmod`; the first one from the left is for a user, the second digit is for a group, and the third digit is for others. By default, `umask` is set to *022*, which gives *644* permissions to all the newly created files and the *755* permissions to all the newly created directories.

The umask setting can be changed either for all users or for individual ones. If you want to set the umask value for all users, you must make sure that the umask setting is entered in the /etc/login.defs configuration file (before, it was entered in the /etc/profile file, but now it is changed to /etc/login.defs). On the other hand, if you would like to apply specific umask settings to only a specific user, you have to edit the profile file that exists under this user's home directory and set the desired umask value there.

Applying quota to user accounts

User quota is another security barrier for servers. They allow administrators to apply a quota restriction to the file and directory creation for users and groups.

To use this feature, you need to perform the following steps:

1. First of all, install the quota software. This is done by using the sudo apt-get install quota command.

2. Secondly, prepare the filesystem to support quota. To do this, you need to add the usrquota option (if you want to apply quota to users) or the grpquota option (for groups) in the options column in the /etc/fstab file for every filesystem in which you want to use quota. Then, remount all the partitions in which quota has been applied by using the following command:

   sudo mount -o remount <partition_name>

3. Next, initialize the quota software. The best way to initialize the quota system is by running the sudo quotacheck -augmv command, which will create the aquota.user and aquota.group files to list all the quota information for actual users.

4. Finally, the real work involves setting up quota for users and groups. This is done via the edquota command. For example, the sudo edquota -u <username> command will open a temporary file for quota for that user in a text editor. This file contains six numbers that specify the quota for all the filesystems on your server. The first one represents the block's number, which is currently being used by the user that you're setting the quota for. The second number is the soft limit for the block's number, while the third number is the hard limit. The fifth and sixth numbers are the equivalents for inodes, which are almost equal to the number of files that this user can create on the filesystem. The first and fourth numbers are just used to record the number of blocks and inodes that are currently being used for this user.

5. After setting up the quota, you need to use the `sudo edquota -t` command to set the grace time that you want to use either in hours, or in days. The grace time is set per filesystem. Therefore, there's no option to specify different grace time settings for different users.

 The initialization step is mandatory in the setting up of quota for a new user; it makes sure that new users are known to the quota system.

After setting up quota, it is useful to monitor it. To do that, you can use the `repquota` command. With the `-aug` options, this command shows the current quota settings for all the users and groups on all the volumes.

Finally, after setting up quotas, don't forget to start the quota service by running the `/etc/init.d/quota start` command.

Once you have set quotas for one user, you may want to apply them to other users. Instead of following the same procedure for all the users on the system, you can use the `edquota -p` command. For example, `sudo edquota -p user1 user2` copies the quotas currently applied for `user1 user` to user `user2`.

The `edquota` command works only with blocks and not bytes, kilobytes, or anything else. So, to set quota properly, you need to know the block size that's currently being used. To find this block size, use the `sudo dumpe2fs <device> | grep "Block size"` command.

Configuring administration tasks with sudo

Ubuntu implements a number of practices out of the box to make the default installation more secure. One of these practices is the disabling of the root account and the use of `sudo` for superuser privileges. The `sudo` program provides a much more robust set of features to increase user privileges as compared to the traditional `su` program.

The `sudo` command's configuration file can be found at `/etc/sudoers`. By default, Ubuntu provides a basic file that allows root users to do anything as any other user, and allows members of the admin group to become root users (the user that you create at the time of installation is automatically added to this group).

The sudo package provides a tool called visudo that you should use whenever you want to make changes to the file. Therefore, to view and edit the /etc/sudoers file, type in the following command:

```
sudo visudo
```

The reason you want to use visudo is that it automatically checks your sudoers file for mistakes. Since a mistake in the sudoers file could potentially lock you out of root access, this syntax check is pretty important. In case you do make a mistake, visudo will tell you about it after you save your settings and exit the page. So, you will have the option of going back and fixing your mistake, exiting without saving, or ignoring its warnings and saving anyway (which is not recommended).

 To edit the file and manage the sudo program in the best possible way, the easiest thing to do is to read and follow the examples in the manual pages. You can access it via the man sudoers command.

Configuring the AppArmor tool

The AppArmor system that is installed by default in Ubuntu Server adds access control to specific system services with an aim to enhance the server security level. AppArmor is based on the security principle of least privileges. For every program, it assigns a series of rules that define a set of files and directories that this program is allowed to handle and explains how to handle them (read only or read write). When an application that is being managed by AppArmor violates these access controls, AppArmor intervenes, prevents it from doing so, and logs the event. There is a huge number of services that include AppArmor profiles by default, and more are being added in every Ubuntu release. In addition to the default profiles, the universe repository has an apparmor-profiles package that you can install to add more profiles for other services. Once you learn the syntax for the AppArmor rules, you can even add your own profiles.

The best way to see how AppArmor works is by using an example program. The MySQL database server is one program that is automatically managed by AppArmor under Ubuntu. So, once the MySQL package is installed, you can use the aa-status program to see that AppArmor is already managing it, as follows:

```
sudo aa-status
apparmor module is loaded.
7 profiles are loaded.
7 profiles are in enforce mode.
  /sbin/dhclient
```

```
/usr/lib/NetworkManager/nm-dhcp-client.action

/usr/lib/NetworkManager/nm-dhcp-helper

/usr/lib/connman/scripts/dhclient-script

/usr/sbin/mysqld

/usr/sbin/named

/usr/sbin/tcpdump
0 profiles are in complain mode.
3 processes have profiles defined.
3 processes are in enforce mode.
   /sbin/dhclient (945)
   /usr/sbin/mysqld (6288)
   /usr/sbin/named (13679)
0 processes are in complain mode.
0 processes are unconfined but have a profile defined.
```

Here you can see that the /usr/sbin/mysqld profile is loaded and is in the enforce mode and that the currently running /usr/sbin/ mysqld process (PID *6288*) is being managed by AppArmor.

AppArmor stores its profiles under the /etc/apparmor.d/ directory, and each filename is derived from the binary file that they manage. For instance, the profile for /usr/sbin/mysqld is located at /etc/apparmor.d/usr.sbin.mysqld. If you look at the contents of the file, you will get an idea of how the AppArmor profiles work and what sort of protection they provide:

```
cat /etc/apparmor.d/usr.sbin.mysqld
# vim: syntax=apparmor
# Last Modified: Tue Jun 19 17:37:30 2007
#include <tunables/global>

/usr/sbin/mysqld {
  #include <abstractions/base>
  #include <abstractions/nameservice>
  #include <abstractions/user-tmp>
  #include <abstractions/mysql>
  #include <abstractions/winbind>

  capability dac_override,
  capability sys_resource,
```

```
    capability setgid,
    capability setuid,

    network tcp,

    /etc/hosts.allow r,
    /etc/hosts.deny r,

    /etc/mysql/** r,
    /usr/lib/mysql/plugin/ r,
    /usr/lib/mysql/plugin/*.so* mr,
    /usr/sbin/mysqld mr,
    /usr/share/mysql/** r,
    /var/log/mysql.log rw,
    /var/log/mysql.err rw,
    /var/lib/mysql/ r,
    /var/lib/mysql/** rwk,
    /var/log/mysql/ r,
    /var/log/mysql/* rw,
    /var/run/mysqld/mysqld.pid rw,
    /var/run/mysqld/mysqld.sock w,
    /run/mysqld/mysqld.pid rw,
    /run/mysqld/mysqld.sock w,

    /sys/devices/system/cpu/ r,

    # Site-specific additions and overrides. See local/README for details.
    #include <local/usr.sbin.mysqld>
}
```

The syntax is pretty straightforward for these files. First, there is a file or a directory path, which is followed by the permissions that are allowed. Globs are also allowed. So for instance, /etc/mysql/** recursively applies the files to all the files in the /etc/mysql directory. A single * will apply files only to files within the current directory.

After modifying an AppArmor profile, you should reload the AppArmor daemon so that the changes take effect. You can do this by using the following command:

```
sudo /etc/init.d/apparmor reload
```

In AppArmor, there are two modes, namely **enforce** and **complain**. In the **enforce** mode, AppArmor actively blocks all the attempts by a program to violate its profile. In the **complain** mode, AppArmor simply logs the attempt but allows it to happen. You can easily change a profile so that it is in the enforce or complain mode by using the `aa-enforce` and `aa-complain` programs respectively.

For example, in case you would like to change the MySQL AppArmor profile from the enforce to complain mode, this profile can perform read and write without restrictions in the profile file, but just those actions will be logged. All that we need to do is run the following command:

```
sudo aa-complain /usr/sbin/mysqld
Setting /usr/sbin/mysqld to complain mode.
```

We can check the AppArmor status after this change, as follows:

```
sudo aa-status
apparmor module is loaded.
7 profiles are loaded.
6 profiles are in enforce mode.
   /sbin/dhclient
   /usr/lib/NetworkManager/nm-dhcp-client.action
   /usr/lib/NetworkManager/nm-dhcp-helper
   /usr/lib/connman/scripts/dhclient-script
   /usr/sbin/named
   /usr/sbin/tcpdump
1 profiles are in complain mode.
   /usr/sbin/mysqld
3 processes have profiles defined.
2 processes are in enforce mode.
   /sbin/dhclient (945)
   /usr/sbin/named (13679)
1 processes are in complain mode.
   /usr/sbin/mysqld (6288)
0 processes are unconfined but have a profile defined.
```

To be able to use the aa-complain and aa-enforce programs, you should first of all install the apparmor-utils package by using the following command:

```
sudo apt-get install apparmor-utils
```

If you want to temporary disable AppArmor (for instance, for some debugging purposes, in case some processes are not working as expected and you are trying to check whether the apparmor profiles are the reason behind it or if it's something else), you just have to run the following command:

```
sudo /etc/init.d/apparmor stop
[ ok ] Stopping apparmor (via systemctl): apparmor.service.
```

Note that running the preceding command will only clear the profile's cache. In case you need to unload the profile, you need to run the following command:

```
sudo /etc/init.d/apparmor teardown
 * Unloading AppArmor profiles [ OK ]
```

Advanced security configuration

In this section, we will discover some advanced security settings that are needed for most Ubuntu servers that are in a production environment, especially when they contain critical services. This advanced configuration is important because it will directly touch the behavior of services besides Ubuntu Server itself.

SSH security enhancement

By definition, SSH is a secure communication protocol, but there are some additional enhancements that we can apply to take this security a step ahead.

Let's start with the default Ubuntu SSH configuration. The /etc/ssh/sshd_config file, which is very secure as it allows authentication keys to be used, uses privilege separation and allows only SSH protocol 2. The only questionable setting is **PermitRootLogin** yes, which defines the option that allows root users to log in via SSH. In our case (Ubuntu Server with the default installation), this setting is useless since the root account is disabled, but in case you would like to enable the root account, you might want to set this option to no and run sudo service ssh reload to save the settings. By following these steps, you force users to log in with their regular accounts and they can perform sudo up command to root in case they need root privileges. This also allows you to prevent a user from being able to guess the root password and gain access.

Another important security enhancement with SSH is the use of key-based authentication instead of passwords. This feature allows you to keep your server safe from brute force attacks. The working of key-based authentication is really simple. It is based on a couple of keys (one public and one private) generated by users. Then, the public key is placed in a special file on the remote server, and the private one must be kept with the user and mustn't be shared with others. When a user logs in, these keys are used to authenticate the user instead of a password. With this approach, and, users can also work more comfortably since they are able to log in to their machines without typing in the password every time. However, in case you want an extra layer of security, you can set a passphrase on your keys as well.

It is relatively simple to set up key-based authentication. In this example, we have a user named abdel on a computer named **abdelmonam2** who wants to set up key authentication on a server named abdelmonam1. The first step is to use the ssh-keygen program to create an RSA public and private key on abdelmonam2. At each prompt, you can press the *Enter* key to accept the defaults, as shown in the following screenshot:

The script creates the keys in the .ssh directory under your home directory, which is /home/abdel/.ssh in this case. The private key and the public key are named id_rsa and id_rsa.pub respectively. It's very important (especially if you chose an empty passphrase) to keep the private key (id_rsa) safe! If anyone else gets access to this file, they can copy it and will be able to log in to a machine that you have set up with this key.

Once you have created the keys, the next step is to copy the `id_rsa.pub` key to the server and then append it to the `~/.ssh/authorized_keys` file. There are a number of ways to do this. The automatic one involves using the following command:

```
ssh-copy-id -i ~/.ssh/id_rsa.pub <username>@<ipaddress>
```

One of the manual ways is to SSH into the remote machine, open `~/.ssh/authorized_keys` with a text editor, and paste in the contents of `id_rsa.pub`.

Once you have the keys set up on a machine, you should be able to log in without a password prompt unless you set a passphrase for your key. If the latter is the case, you will need to type it. After your keys work, you might want to disable SSH password authentication altogether. Just make sure that your SSH keys work first, or you could lock yourself out! To disable password authentication, edit `/etc/ssh/sshd_config` and locate the line that says `#PasswordAuthentication yes`. Uncomment this line and set it to no, as follows:

```
PasswordAuthentication no
```

Finally, run `sudo service sshd reload` to load the new change.

 The default is a *2048 bit* key. You can increase this to *4096 bits* with the `-b` flag (increasing the bits makes it harder to crack the key by brute force methods), as follows:

```
ssh-keygen -t rsa -b 4096
```

Another method that allows you to prevent SSH brute force attacks, especially when you can not disable password authentication for one reason or another, is the use of the `denyhosts` package. This package monitors for failed SSH logins. When a host attempts to log in either as a user that doesn't exist, or too many times, that host is added to `/etc/hosts.deny` and blocked from future SSH access.

Configuring firewalls

One of the most common ways of protecting machines on a network is with a firewall. Essentially, a firewall gives you the ability to restrict access to services over the network. With a firewall, you can limit access to SSH, for instance, to hosts only within your internal network, while allowing HTTP access to everyone.

Historically, the firewall rules in Linux need to be set with a long and complicated set of `iptables` commands (also known as the `iptables` rules). This complexity is a weakness because one of the main security principles is to do things in a simple way. Luckily for Ubuntu administrators, there is now a simpler tool named `ufw`, which aims to simplify firewall administration by providing a frontend to the `iptables` commands.

The `ufw` program is installed by default on Ubuntu Server, but it is disabled; you need to enable it before you start adding rules.

The basic set of `ufw` commands is pretty straightforward. If you run `ufw -h`, you will get a help page that describes the main `ufw` commands, but if you want the entire syntax information, type in `man ufw` to read the entire manual page. First of all, let's identify the main commands and then see some examples:

- You can enable and disable `ufw` by using `sudo ufw enable` and `sudo ufw disable` respectively.

- Check the `ufw` status by using `sudo ufw status`; the same command will list all the rules in case `ufw` is enabled.

- You can also set the default policy of your firewall. A very important command that you need to consider is the `default` command. This command defines the default policy of your firewall, as in whether all the packets are allowed or denied by default. The general consensus is that a firewall is more secure if you deny all packets by default and then enable services as needed. That way, in case you start a new service (or worse, a user starts a service) and you forget to set firewall rules for it, it will be blocked by default. So, to deny all packets by default, type in `sudo ufw default deny`. To allow all packets by default, type in `sudo ufw default allow`. Note that `ufw` will deny all packets by default unless you change the settings.

- You can configure the logging function to trace anything that it blocks, along with anything against your default policy. To enable logging, type in `sudo ufw logging on`, and to disable it, type in `sudo ufw logging off`.

- A basic `ufw` rule takes a port or service as an argument. To open port 53 (used for DNS servers), you would run `sudo ufw allow 53`.

- The `ufw` command also accepts service names that are defined in the `/etc/services` file instead of specific ports. If you look in the `/etc/services` file, you will see that port 53 TCP and UDP is set to the domain service. So, another way of stating this rule is `sudo ufw allow domain`.

- You can also specify the transport protocol. An example of this is `sudo ufw allow 53/udp`.

- You can also set a specific subnet that is allowed to access the server. Here's an example command that is used to limit web access (port 80) to just the *192.168.1.0* network:

  `sudo ufw allow proto tcp from 192.168.1.0/24 to any port 80`

- Even if you deny all packets by default, there may be circumstances in which you may also add a deny rule. For instance, let's say that you are running an external SMTP (e-mail) server and you see that a host inside your network at *192.168.1.111* appears to be infected with a virus and is flooding your e-mail server with invalid messages. To block just that IP address, you will execute the following command:

  `sudo ufw deny proto tcp from 192.168.1.111 to any port 25`

- In case you want to block all the packets from that host and not just the SMTP, you wouldn't need to define the proto and to arguments:

  `sudo ufw deny from 192.168.1.111`

- Later on, once the virus has been removed and the host is back to normal, you can remove the rule with the help of the following command:

  `sudo ufw delete deny proto tcp from 192.168.1.111 to any port 25`

- Alternatively, in case you dropped all the packets from the host, the following command will remove it:

  `sudo ufw delete deny from 192.168.1.111`

 Be careful when using `ufw` while you are connected via SSH because enabling `ufw` with its default action of denying all packets will close your SSH connection and isolate your server. The best thing to do when you start configuring `ufw` and before enabling it or adding any other rules is to add the following rule:

`sudo ufw allow ssh`

Now, let's have a look at a couple of examples:

- For a DNS server, we need to allow DNS packets and deny the others, of course after allowing SSH, and at the end, enable `ufw` and check its status. The following is a sequence of commands. Take care of the order; it matters a lot:

  ```
  sudo ufw allow ssh
  sudo ufw allow domain
  sudo ufw default deny
  sudo ufw enable
  sudo ufw status
  ```

- The following is another example where we have more than one service. This is the web server, where in general, we should allow `http (80)` and `https (443)` access:

  ```
  sudo ufw allow ssh
  sudo ufw allow www
  sudo ufw allow https
  sudo ufw default deny
  sudo ufw enable
  sudo ufw status
  ```

Backuping and restoring

The tools and procedures that we saw in this chapter until now allow us to raise the server security level and enhance the ability to block attacks, but what if we are being attacked? In some cases, we can investigate and clean up the system, but in most cases, neither the time nor the means allow us to do that, and the best solution is to restore a healthy backed up image of the system. The backup and restore procedures solve not only problems related to attacks, but also problems related to data loss that are caused by human mistakes or physical accidents such as a server room fire.

In the following section, you will discover how to perform a backup/restore of Ubuntu Server in more than one way with more than one tool.

The principles of backup

There are a number of principles that should guide you when you choose your backup strategy. Most of these are common sense but bear repeating:

- Back up your data to a separate system
- Test your backups
- RAID is not a substitute for backups
- Create full and incremental backup schedules
- Decide how often you need to back up
- Archive your backups

Drive imaging

An image is a complete bit-for-bit copy of a drive. So, once you image a drive, you will get an identical image of the original drive.

 When imaging a drive, it's important that the drive is not in use. In case the drive changes when imaging it, you will not be able to guarantee that the image is consistent. So, be sure that the filesystems on a drive are unmounted.

Ubuntu Server uses the classic UNIX imaging tool named dd. Its working process is simple—it reads an input file bit by bit and copies it to an output file bit by bit. If you had two drives of identical size, say /dev/sda and /dev/sdb, use the following command to image sda to sdb:

```
sudo dd if=/dev/sda of=/dev/sdb
```

The dd tool also works with files as input and output arguments instead of drivers. So it's better to image our target in a file instead of a driver so that we can copy it easily in a transportable device such as a USB driver or send it to a remote file server.

For example, if you want to back up the sda partition in an image file under a USB driver mounted under /media/myUSB/, all you need to do is execute the following command:

```
sudo dd if=/dev/sda of=/media/myUSB/sda-image.img
```

To restore this image, just reverse the two arguments. Here are the commands to restore the two previous examples:

```
sudo dd if=/dev/sdb of=/dev/sda
```

```
sudo dd if=/media/myUSB/sda-image.img of=/dev/sda
```

You can also image individual partitions. This can be useful because you can easily mount the image loopback and read through them. First, let's image a partition on /dev/sda, as follows:

```
sudo dd if=/dev/sda1 of=/media/myUSB/sda1-image.img
```

Now, you can create a directory named /mnt/temp and use the loop mount option to mount this image, as follows:

```
sudo mkdir /mnt/temp
```

```
sudo mount loop /media/myUSB/sda1-image.img /mnt/temp
```

This is handy when you need to recover only a few files from an image. You can browse /mnt/temp like any other filesystem and copy individual files or entire directories from it.

We can directly back up an image of a given driver to a remote server by using SSH. For example, to transfer /dev/sda from the local machine over the network to *192.168.1.200* and dump the image at /media/MyBackupData/sda-image.img, you would type in the following code:

```
sudo dd if=/dev/sda | ssh username@192.168.1.200 \
```

```
"cat > /media/MyBackupData/sda-image.img"
```

To restore this image, use the following code:

```
ssh username@192.168.1.200 "cat /media/MyBackupData/sda-image.img" \
sudo dd of=/dev/sda
```

Database backups

For the most part, backing up a system is as easy as creating a copy of its files. However, on a database system, things aren't quite that simple. A database often won't commit changes to disk immediately. So, if you simply make a copy of the database files, the database itself might be in an inconsistent state. When you restore it, you can't necessarily guarantee that it is an uncorrupted copy.

The solution to this problem is to use tools included with the database to provide a consistent dump of the complete database to a file that you can back up. In the following section, you will learn how to use the tools provided for the MySQL databases in Ubuntu. A similar procedure is applied to other databases, depending on their own dumping tools.

The tool that MySQL uses to create a backup of its database is called **mysqldump**. This tool dumps an entire database or databases to the screen. Most people then redirect the output to a file or pipe it to a tool such as gzip to compress it first. For instance, if your user had a database called mySite, here is how should will back it up:

```
mysqldump mySite > mySite_backup.sql
```

If you wanted to compress the database as it was dumped, put a pipe to gzip in the middle, as follows:

```
mysqldump MySite | gzip > MySite_backup.sql.gz
```

Now, if you want to back up more than one database, there are two main ways to do it. The first way is to use the --databases argument, followed by a space-separated list of databases that you need to back up. The other method is to use the --all-databases argument, which backs up everything, as follows:

```
mysqldump --all-databases > all_databases_backup.sql
```

In case you set passwords for the MySQL users, you should provide them by using the -u and -p options to get this command working. For example, for the root user with a mySecret password, run the following command:

```
mysqldump --all-databases -u root -pmySecret \ >
all_databases_backup.sql
```

The preceding command will back up all the databases as the root user is using an insecure password. I gave this example only to say that while this option works, it is insecure. The reason is that the full list of arguments, including the password, will be visible to all the users on the system who run the ps command. A better method is to use -p without specifying a password:

```
mysqldump --all-databases -u root -p \ >
all_databases_backup.sql
```

When you specify `-p` without a password, `mysqldump` behaves like the `mysql` command and prompts you to enter a password. This provides good security, but it of course also means that you have to enter the password manually. Most people who back up their MySQL databases set up a `cron` job to do it at night. The way that MySQL recommends to solve this problem is to add the password to the client section in the `~/.my.cnf` file for the user performing the backups. If you already don't have a `~/.my.cnf` file, create a new one and add the following text in it:

```
[client]
password=mypassword
```

Replace `mypassword` with the password that your user will use to log in. Once you set up this file, you don't need to specify the `-p` option anymore, because `mysqldump` will pick up the password from this file. The downside here is that this password is in a plain-text file on the system. So, you will want to set its permissions so that only your user can see it:

```
chmod 400 ~/.my.cnf
```

To restore a backup on MySQL, use the `mysql` command-line tool and point it at your backup. For instance, to back up the `mySite` database to `mySite_backup.sql`, execute the following command:

```
mysql mySite < mySite_backup.sql
```

Instead, in case you are backing up a number of databases, just execute the following command:

```
mysql < multiple_database_backup.sql
```

To restore all the databases, you need to log in as the root user. In case you set a root password, you must use the `-p` option (unless you set up a `.my.cnf` file; in that case, you can leave out `-p`), as follows:

```
mysql -u root -p < all_databases.sql
```

Backup tools

There are a lot of backup tools that we can use to backup and easily restore Ubuntu Server. Some of them use CLI and others use GUI; some are free, while others come with a paid license. They also differ according to the backup mode, which can be **full** (the tool backs up all the files in the backup target), **incremental** (the tool backs up all the files that have been changed since the last backup), or **differential** (the tool backs up all the files that have been changed since the last full backup).

Here's a comparison of some of the well-known tools:

Tool name	Interface	Remarks
Areca Backup	GUI	This is a great backup software that works locally or with FTP, is written in Java, has a very intuitive GTK graphical interface, and provides possibilities of complete restorations and file search.
Bacula	GUI	This is a professional open source backup software. It saves the contents of a PC or a PC with multiple networks. Bacula has a lot of features. But it requires you to have advanced knowledge in terms of backups.
BackInTime	GUI	This is a very simple backup tool that is available for Linux. The backup is done by taking "snapshots" of a set of directories. Currently, there are two available GUIs, namely Gnome and KDE. This solution is one of the few tools that let you save the file on a remote server via SSH and store it in an encrypted form. It is possible to save the file on a dedicated server without concern for the security of its data once it's stored.
BackupPC	GUI	This is a very powerful tool that can be used to back up multiple clients (Linux or Windows). BackupPC is used to save a set of machines. It has a web interface to configure and initiate backups or restore files. It is also possible to back up databases. BackupPC can automatically save the directories on networked computers at regular time intervals. It can also do much more.
Déjà Dup	GUI	This is a simple backup utility and a GUI tool for duplicity. It allows you to create backups in a local directory, on servers (SSH/FTP/HTTP), or on the Cloud. It also allows you to encrypt the saved files and schedule automatic backups.
LuckyBackup	GUI	This is a simple tool with the power of rsync in a friendly interface. It offers features such as simple or advanced mode, restore, simulation, the remote operation, superuser mode, profiles, and planning.
SBackup	GUI	This is a simple tool that you can use easily, and it is powerful. It allows you to perform an incremental backup but not a differential backup.

Tool name	Interface	Remarks
Backup-Manager	CLI	With this tool, backup files are stored locally in archives and can be exported on a server (FTP, SSH, rsync, and so on) or burned on a CD/DVD.
Duplicity	CLI	This tool performs backups by creating TAR archives that are encrypted with GnuPG. These archives are then sent to a local or remote backup directory. The supported remote protocols are FTP, SSH/SCP, Rsync, WebDAV/ WebDAVs, and Amazon S3.
Rsync	CLI	Rsync (for remote synchronization) is a file synchronization software. It is frequently used to implement remote backup systems. Rsync works unidirectionally, which means that it synchronizes, copies, or updates source data (local or remote) to a destination (local or remote) by transferring the bytes of the files that have been modified.
Unison	CLI	Unison is a synchronization software. Unlike Rsync, it displays bidirectional synchronization.

There are also some specific backup tools that are dedicated to partition cloning. The following are two such famous tools for Ubuntu:

Tool name	Interface	Remarks
Clonezilla	GUI	This is a free equivalent of Norton Ghost or Acronis True Image. It allows you to create an image backup of a hard disk or partition and then restore it.
Partclone	CLI	It is used to backup a partition. It is somehow the equivalent of Norton Ghost. It can be installed on a live usb to save your system.

Now, let's take as an example the powerful backup tool named **BackupPC**. To install it, you need to run the following command:

```
sudo apt-get install backuppc
```

You will be asked for some information related to the mail server (postfix) and the web server that you wish to use (in our case, it is Apache), as shown in the following screenshot. In the end, you will get a message indicating the URL needed to manage BackupPC and the needed credentials to log in to the system:

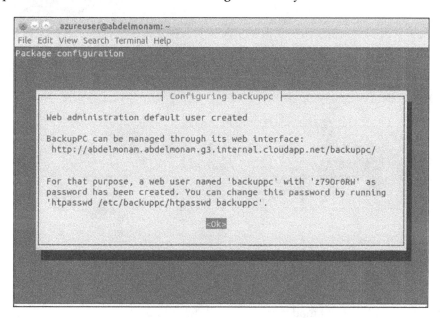

To activate the new configuration, you need to run the following command:

```
sudo service apache2 restart
```

Then, you can start using BackupPC via a web browser by using either the URL given in the message, or the server IP address followed by /backuppc/. You will be asked for login credentials, as shown in the following screenshot. After entering them, you will get a a good interface that is easy to use with a very rich documentation:

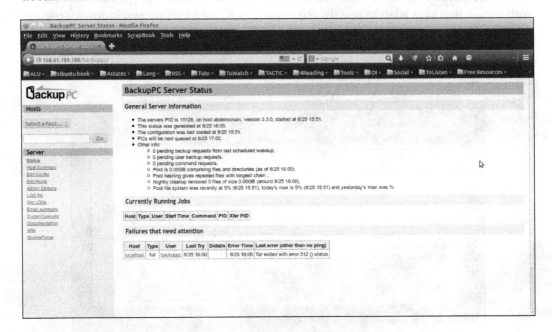

 You can find out more information on how to use BackupPC in both GUI and CLI modes at https://help.ubuntu.com/community/ BackupPC.

Summary

In this chapter, we focused on a very important subject related to Ubuntu Server, namely security management. We covered the basic and advanced security features inside Ubuntu Server and explored how to use them to enhance a system's security level. Then, we got an overview of the backup/restore operations for Ubuntu Server.

In the next chapter, we will concentrate on one of the hottest IT subjects nowadays, which is virtualization and Cloud computing based on Ubuntu Server.

5

Virtualization and Cloud Computing inside the Ubuntu Server

Virtualization and Cloud computing are some of the hottest topics in system administration communities nowadays. They give system administrators the possibility to run more servers on the same hardware and use resources in a reliable manner. The Cloud concept, which is already based on virtualization, provides much more benefits, especially via security and new business models such as SaaS, PaaS, and IaaS.

Ubuntu provides a good set of virtualization and Cloud computing platforms. In this chapter, we will have a look at how the Ubuntu Server handles the most well known platforms:

- In the first section, we will focus on virtualization. We will discover how to manage three big virtualization programs, namely KVM, XenServer, and Docker.

- In the second section, we will take a look at the Cloud capabilities provided by the Ubuntu Server.

Virtualization

There are a number of different virtualization technologies available under the Ubuntu Server. In this section, we will discover the virtualization concept in general with its different technologies and approach. Then, we will study some of the most popular virtualization programs, such as **Kernel-based Virtual Machine (KVM)**, XenServer and Docker, with one program from each technology.

An introduction to virtualization

Virtualization is used to run one or more operating systems / applications as a simple software on one or more computers/servers instead of not being able to install more than one operating system per machine. These **virtual machines** are called **VMs**, **environments**, and even **VEs**. The virtualization of **operating systems (OS)** is a technique that allows you to run multiple OSes simultaneously on a single computer as if they were working on separate computers.

The benefits of virtualization

Virtualization has several advantages. The following are some of its benefits:

- You can use a different OS without restarting your computer to use programs that do not natively work on Ubuntu

- You can also use devices that don't work with Ubuntu but that can work with other OSs

- You can perform testing under the operating systems without jeopardizing a stable environment

- You can also perform software testing in controlled, isolated and secure environments

- You can transport OS from one computer to another using a virtual machine running on a computer with a compatible hypervisor

Individuals and **Small and Medium Enterprise (SMEs)** / **Small and Medium Industries (SMIs)** will generally be more interested in running two different OSes at the same time to run software that are compatible with one hypervisor but not the other. Large companies are increasingly using virtualization to save space in server rooms, simplify installations, facilitate restarts after incidents, and of course, develop secure and reliable business networks.

Different techniques of virtualization

The main aspect of the virtualization concept is an entity called **hypervisor**. A hypervisor is a software, firmware, or hardware that creates and runs virtual machines. The machine that runs a hypervisor is called the host machine, and every virtual machine that runs on a hypervisor is called a guest machine. There are two types of hypervisors that we will see in this section. Besides a hypervisor, there is another main piece of virtualization concept that takes more than one name. Some call it an **isolator**, while others call it a **container**, **virtualization engine**, or even an **operating-system-level virtualization**. In our case, we will call it an isolator. We will discover this, as well as the two hypervisor types, in this section.

Type 1 hypervisor

This type of hypervisor is also called a **native** or **bare-metal hypervisor**. It runs directly on a host's hardware, and it handles the hardware directly and manages the guest OS. An example of this hypervisor type is the **XenServer**.

We can model it by using the following schema:

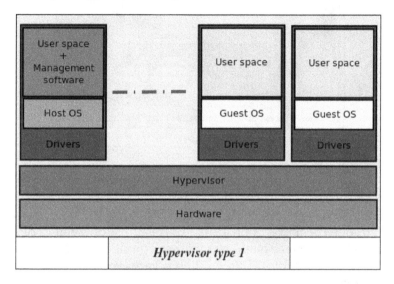

Hypervisor type 1

Type 2 hypervisor

This type of hypervisor is also called a **hosted hypervisor**. It runs on the host OS just like any other software. It provides an emulation of the hardware level to guest systems. An example of this hypervisor type is **Oracle VirtualBox**.

 Some virtualization programs, such as KVM, can't be easily classified into either of the two types. **KVM** is a kernel module that converts the host OS to a type 1 hypervisor, but at the same time, the host OS always works as a general-purpose OS that runs other applications that compete for VM resources. Therefore, KVM can also be categorized as a type 2 hypervisor.

We can model type 2 hypervisor by using the following schema:

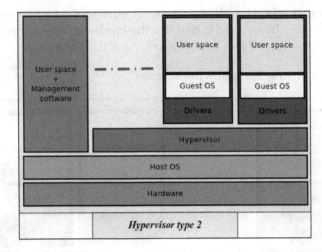

An isolator

An isolator is a piece of software that is used to isolate applications' executions in what are called contexts or execution areas. An isolator allows you to run the same application in a multi-instance mode several times (multiple execution instances) even if it was not designed for it. This solution is very efficient because of the little overhead (the time spent by a system to do more than just manage itself). Note that virtualized environments are not completely isolated. The performance is always a key factor. However, we cannot really talk about OS virtualization. We can model it by using the following schema:

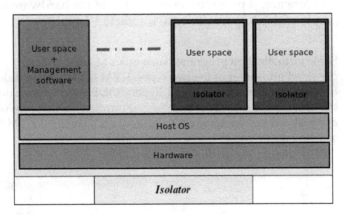

The different approaches towards virtualization

Before starting a virtualization project, it is mandatory to understand the two main approaches in this field—**full virtualization** and **paravirtualization**. Both XenServer and KVM offer these two approaches. Therefore, you need to know the differences between them very well, and this is what we will explain in the following sections.

Paravirtualization

The paravirtualization approach requires a modified version of the guest OS, that generates special instructions that can be easily handled by the hypervisor, which simply interprets and passes them to the physical hardware.

In this case, the guest OS knows that it is virtualized. As a result, it will generate instructions that are best optimized for use in a VE and don't need to be translated first.

Full virtualization

The other approach is full virtualization, which allows you to use an unmodified OS as a guest. One of its disadvantages is that it requires special hardware support, which is something that is nowadays provided as a special feature in modern CPUs (both AMD and Intel processors). Thanks to this built-in support within the server's CPU, fully virtualized machines can work as efficiently as possible in spite of the fact that the instructions coming from the virtualized OS first need to be translated by the hypervisor.

KVM (Kernel-based Virtual Machine)

In this section, we will discover the default virtualization technology that is actually supported by Ubuntu. Named **KVM** (**Kernel-based Virtual Machine**), this virtualization technology is a free software with support built into the Linux kernel. This software takes advantage of the virtualization support that is built into the Intel and AMD processors and allows you to run a number of different distributions and OSes as **VMs** (**virtual machines**) on a single host.

Prerequisites

Before starting the installation process, you should verify that your computer supports virtualization. To check this, you need to run the `kvm-ok` command, which is a part of the `cpu-checker` package. Therefore, you first of all need to install this package and then invoke the command by using the following code:

```
sudo apt-get install cpu-checker
sudo kvm-ok
```

Then, check the result and verify that you got the following result:

```
INFO: Your CPU does not support KVM extensions
KVM acceleration can NOT be used
```

This means that you should look for another computer. However, you may get something like this:

```
INFO: /dev/kvm does not exist
HINT: sudo modprobe kvm_intel
INFO: Your CPU supports KVM extensions
KVM acceleration can be used
```

Alternatively, you may get something like this:

```
INFO: /dev/kvm exists
KVM acceleration can be used
```

This means that you can move on to the next section.

Sometimes your CPU supports virtualization, but you may get a message saying that it can't. In such cases, most of the time, virtualization is disabled in the BIOS. Therefore, you will have to enable it from there. All that you need to do is restart your computer and access the BIOS by using the appropriate function key (it appears on the screen for a few seconds just after the boot; most of the time, you need to use *F12*). From the BIOS screen that appears, look for something such as a CPU or performance heading and select it. Then, look for a virtualization selection, such as **Intel Virtualization Technology**, and enable it. Save your changes and reboot.

Configuring the KVM networking

There are two main ways that can be used to set up the network for your VMs. The default networking setup provides a private network under *192.168.122.0/24*. A DHCP server will hand out the rest of the IPs. Alternatively, you can set up static IPs for your VM. The IP of the KVM host is *192.168.122.1*. VMs communicate with the outside world via this gateway by using **NAT** (**Network Address Translation**). This works fine, especially for VMs on a desktop, but since we are talking about servers here, my assumption is that you want machines outside the KVM host to be able to communicate with your VMs. While you can certainly set up some iptables DNAT rules and forward traffic back in, this solution doesn't scale very well. The real solution is to set up a bridged network so that your VMs appear to be on the same network as that of your host.

It is relatively simple to set up the `br0` bridge interface on Ubuntu. Essentially, you need to identify the interface over which you want to bridge traffic (probably `eth0` or possibly `bond0` if you set up bonding), transfer all of its configuration to `br0` along with a few extra bridge options, and change the original interface to the manual mode. It will make more sense when you see the examples. Consider an instance where I had a DHCP set up for `eth0`, and my old configuration in `/etc/network/interfaces` looked like this:

```
auto eth0
iface eth0 inet dhcp
```

Then, my new configuration will look like this:

```
auto eth0
iface eth0 inet manual
auto br0
iface br0 inet dhcp
bridge_ports eth0
bridge_fd 9
bridge_hello 2
bridge_maxage 12
bridge_stp off
```

> For more information about network bridging on an Ubuntu Server, you can visit `https://help.ubuntu.com/community/NetworkConnectionBridge`.

Note that I changed the `inet` mode for `eth0` from `dhcp` to `manual`. If `eth0` has a static IP configured, I can just transfer the configuration to `br0` instead. Let's take a look at the following configuration:

```
auto eth0
iface eth0 inet static
address 192.168.0.5
network 192.168.0.0
netmask 255.255.255.0
broadcast 192.168.0.255
gateway 192.168.0.1
```

This will go to the following configuration:

```
auto eth0
iface eth0 inet manual
auto br0
iface br0 inet static
address 192.168.0.5
network 192.168.0.0
netmask 255.255.255.0
broadcast 192.168.0.255
gateway 192.168.0.1
bridge_ports eth0
bridge_fd 9
bridge_hello 2
bridge_maxage 12
bridge_stp off
```

Once I have set up `/etc/network/interfaces` to have the bridge, I then restart the network by using the following command:

```
sudo /etc/init.d/networking restart
```

 To know more about advanced network configurations for KVM on the Ubuntu Server, you can take a look at the community page at `https://help.ubuntu.com/community/KVM/Networking` and the official Ubuntu documentation at `https://wiki.ubuntu.com/KvmWithBridge`.

The KVM installation

To perform the KVM virtualization, you need to install some additional software besides KVM. The following software components need to be added:

- `libvirt`: This provides an interface to the virtualization hardware
- `qemu`: This emulates the PC hardware to virtual machines
- `bridge-utils`: This offers a way to bridge networking from virtual machines through the host

To install the basic software needed for the KVM virtualization, run the following command:

```
sudo apt-get install libvirt-bin kvm bridge-utils qemu-common
qemu-kvm qemu-utils
```

Note that to manage this set of programs, you will mainly use the **command language interpreter (CLI)** commands. In case you would like to use a GUI to manage your VMs, there is the famous `virt-manager` graphical software that does the job. Note that you need to either have a graphical environment installed, or connect to your server by using SSH with the -x option. There is another solution — install `virt-manager` on another desktop/laptop that has a graphical environment and then use it to remotely manage your VMs by using the following command:

```
virt-manager -c qemu+ssh://root@your-server-ip-or-name/system
```

To install `virt-manager`, execute the following command:

```
sudo apt-get install virt-manager
```

With `virt-manager` installed, you now have a choice of managing virtual machines from a graphical interface or from the command line. Next, you want to make sure that the user account from which you want to manage virtualization is configured to do so.

> After finishing the installation process, you should add the user whom you wish to manage the virtualization of the `libvirtd` group by using the following command:
>
> ```
> sudo adduser <user_name> libvirtd
> ```

Finally, reboot your server, log in as the user, and check whether the virtualization services are running. At this point, you can start managing your VE.

Managing virtual machines

If you want to manage a VE by using the `virt-manager` graphic tool, simply run the `virt-manager` command, and you will get an intuitive, easy-to-use GUI. You can customize it by editing the **preferences** sub-menu of the **edit** menu. You also need to check the connection details via the **edit** menu to customize advanced settings, such as networks and storage, as shown in the following screenshot:

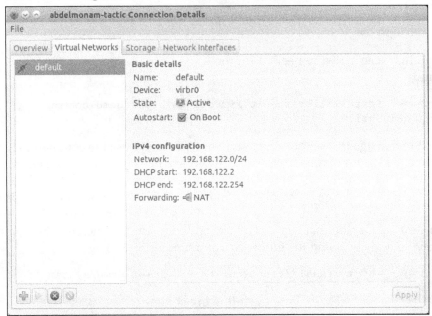

Then, you can start creating and managing your VMs; it is very easy and intuitive.

On the other hand, if you choose to work using CLI, you should master the options that can be used with the main virtualization commands. To get started, you can use the `virt-install` command to install a virtual machine. With `virt-clone`, you can clone an existing virtual image. To manage VMs, you can use the `virsh` command to list information about VMs as well as start, stop, and reboot them.

Note that before creating a VM by using `virt-install`, you need to create the storage image beforehand. One way to do that is by using the `qemu-img` command. For example, the following command will create a 20 GB storage image named `ubuntuserver` of the `qcow2` type under the `/media/Data` directory:

```
sudo qemu-img create -f qcow2 /media/Data/ubuntuserver.qcow2 20G
```

After performing this step, you can create a VM. Here's an example of a `virt-install` command line that creates an Ubuntu virtual machine. This command incorporates many of the options that you would need to click on or fill in on the `virt-manager` window. Note that this command incorporates the image that we created earlier in this section by using the `qemu-img` command:

```
virt-install --connect qemu:///system --name ubuntu_server15.04 \
--ram 1024 --disk path=/media/Data/ubuntuserver.qcow2,format=qcow2 \
--network=bridge:virbr0,model=virtio --vnc --os-type=linux \
--cdrom /media/Data/ISOs/ ubuntu-15.04-server-amd64.iso \
--noautoconsole --keymap=en-us
```

To see the signification of each of these options (and much more) that can be used with the `virt-install` command, you need to check the `virt-install` man page (type man `virt-install`).

Once the `virt-install` command starts, you can open an application from the desktop to see the progress of the installation. The `virt-manager` and `virt-viewer` commands are among those commands that you can use to view your VM's console. After the VM is installed, you can manage your VMs by using the `virsh` command.

The `virsh` command provides a good way to manage your VMs after they are created. You can use `virsh` to see which VMs are running. Then, you can start, stop, pause, and otherwise manage them. There are many alternatives to the `virsh` command that you can use to manage VMs. Refer to the `virsh` man page (type man `virsh`) for details.

XenServer

The second virtualization platform that we will discuss is the famous **XenServer**. Since version 7.10, XenServer was supported by the Ubuntu Server, but starting from version 8.04, Canonical made the decision to go with KVM as the default solution for virtualization in the Ubuntu Server.

In this section, we will discuss how to set up the Ubuntu Server as a host for the Xen virtualization. We will also learn how to install guests in a Xen environment. Just before starting the hands-on part of this section, let's discover a bit of the Xen terminology. In Xen, there's no difference between a host and a guest OS. This is because the words "host" and "guest" suggest a hierarchical relation that doesn't exist (take a look at the type 1 hypervisor model described in the first section of this chapter). So, Xen talks about domains. There is the **domain 0** OS (which can be compared to the host OS in other virtualization technologies) and the other OSes (which can be compared to guest OSs).

These other OSes are referred to as **domain U** machines. The **domain 0** OS (or just **dom0**) is the first OS that loads on a physical machine, and it has specific responsibilities in the Xen environment, including driver management. The **domain U** (or just **domU**) machines are virtualized machines that do not have a special responsibility with regard to virtualization.

Prerequisites

The hardware supported by Linux is available for Xen (it should just be compatible with the kernel). By default, Xen supports all the operating systems that are modified to operate within it, which is called paravirtualization. Xen supports unmodified operating systems as well through hardware virtualization, which is called full virtualization. However, here we must use a CPU that has hardware virtualization support (Intel VT and AMD-V). There is more than one way of verifying this point. For example, we can check the flags set for the CPU in /proc/cpuinfo. By using the egrep command, we can search that file for Intel-VT support (vmx) or AMD-V support (svm) by using the following command:

```
egrep "(svm|vmx)" /proc/cpuinfo
```

The output of this command is shown in the following screenshot:

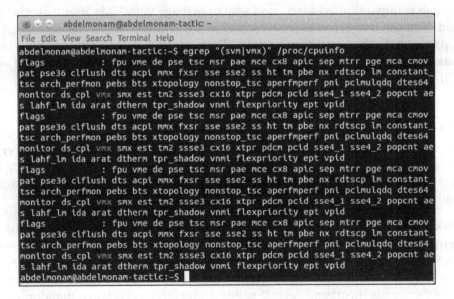

Another way of checking this point is by using the `xm dmesg` command to see an overview of all the features that are relevant to the Xen virtualization, as follows:

```
sudo xm dmesg | grep VMX
(XEN) HVM: VMX enabled
(XEN) VMX: MSR intercept bitmap enabled
```

If you don't get a result, your CPU doesn't support virtualization, which means that you can't virtualize unmodified OSes.

Installing XenServer

Installing XenServer is quite easy for Ubuntu. All that you have to do is run the following command:

```
sudo apt-get install xen-hypervisor
```

Then, restart your system and from **GRand Unified Bootloader** (**GRUB**), choose the entry containing XenServer.

After rebooting, check whether or not you are using the good kernel. Run the `sudo uname -a` command and verify that `xen` is present in the result. Also, verify that `dom0` is launched by using the `sudo xm list` command.

Verify that the network is properly configured. The `ifconfig` command must return at least three interfaces, namely `lo` (the loopback system), `eth0` (the bridge that is no longer your network interface but is the image for `domU`), and `peth0` (the network interface). If this is not the case, edit the `/etc/xen/xend-config.sxp` file and ensure that you have the following lines uncommented:

```
(network-script network-bridge)
(vif-script vif-bridge)
```

Don't forget to restart the Xen daemon after modifying this script by using the following command:

```
service xend restart
```

The `Xen` daemon is responsible for virtual network infrastructure management.

The networking concept in a XenServer environment

Xen has a specific network environment that is different from other VEs. Every domain (starting from dom0) has its own virtual drivers that serve as a network card; they are simply named eth0, eth1 and so on. Inside the dom0 OS, you will find a logical representation (logical interfaces) for these virtual drivers, with the name having the vifx.y pattern, where x represents the ID of the virtualized OS (the **U** in **domU**) and y represents the number of the virtualized network board (starting from 0).

For example, the first network card (eth0) in dom0 is represented by vif0.0, the second network card (eth1) in dom3 is represented by vif3.1, and so on.

Continuing with the exploring of this concept, in the dom0 system, all the vif interfaces are attached to the virtual bridge (called xenbr0), that behaves like a real switch. Next, this bridge communicates with peth0, which is the representation of the physical network card, that finally talks directly to the network board in your server. The following figure is a graphical representation of how all of this is organized:

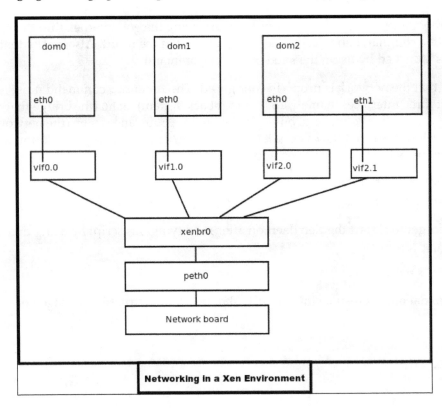

After creating the virtual network, you have to add the `max_loop=64` line loop in the `/etc/modules` file. This is mandatory as you need to ensure that you can create enough virtual disks for your virtual machines. A reboot is needed to confirm that this new setting works before you start creating virtual machines.

Managing virtual machines

Like KVM, XenServer can also be managed by using either GUI or CLI. For GUI, there is a multitude of tools. The following are some of these tools:

- **Virt-manager**: We had a look at this in the KVM section. This works very well if you wish to create and manage XenServer VMs.

- **OpenXenManager**: This is a dedicated GUI that can be used to manage Xen. You can install it by using the following command:

  ```
  sudo apt-get install openxenmanager
  ```

- **XCP Project Kronos**: XCP stands for **Xen Cloud Platform**. To install this, you have to add the `ppa:ubuntu-xen-org/xcp1` PPA to your source list (see *Chapter 2, Configuring and Administering Ubuntu Server*, to learn how to do this), update the package list, and finally run `sudo apt-get install xcp-storage-managers`.

- **xen-tools**: You can install this by using the following command:

  ```
  sudo apt-get install xen-tools
  ```

In the following part of this section, we will concentrate on CLI tools. The native way of doing this is by creating a storage image by using a tool, such as `dd`, as discussed in the backup/restore section in *Chapter 4, Security with Ubuntu*. Next, you need to create a configuration file for the guest system, which will contain all the settings used by the guest system (RAM, hard disk, and so on), and create a VM based on that `config` file by using the following command:

```
sudo xm create -c <path_to_the_conf_file>
```

The `xm create` command can also be used without a `config` file, as follows:

```
sudo xm create /dev/null ramdisk=initrd.img \
kernel=/boot/vmlinuz-2.6.12.6-xenU \
name=ramdisk vif='' vcpus=1 \
memory=64 root=/dev/ram0
```

The `xm` manual contains a lot of helpful information if you wish to use `xm`. Take a look at it before you start using `xm`.

An introduction to Docker

Docker is a famous program that automates and simplifies the deployment of applications and services inside software containers. It is one of the best tools that is classified under the isolator category (see the first section of this chapter). Docker is based on an additional layer of abstraction and automation of an operating-system-level virtualization (also known as the isolator). It was supported by the Ubuntu Server from its 14.04 release. According to an industry analyst firm named 451 Research:

> *"Docker is a tool that can package an application and its dependencies in a virtual container that can run on any Linux server. This helps enable flexibility and portability on where the application can run, whether on premises, public cloud, private cloud, bare metal, etc."*

How Docker works

As discussed earlier, an isolator provides an environment (containers) to run processes in isolation. This is exactly what's done by Docker in a lightweight manner by implementing a high-level API that uses resource isolation features provided by the Linux kernel (such as kernel namespaces, cgroups, and so on) to allow separate containers to run inside a single Linux instance.

Unlike a virtual machine, a Docker container does not require a separate OS. Instead, it uses resource isolation (CPU, memory, block I/O, network, and so on) to isolate an application's view of the operating system. There are two ways that can be used by Docker to access the Linux kernel's virtualization features. The first way involves directly using the `libcontainer` library, which has been available since Docker 0.9. The second way requires you to indirectly use a multitude of tools, such as `libvirt`, `systemd-nspawn`, and **LXC (Linux Containers)**.

The resource isolation and service restrictions that result from the use of containers provide an almost completely private view of the operating system. Therefore, every container has its own process ID space, file system structure, and network interfaces. By adding a few additional constraints for each container to use only a defined amount of resources, such as CPU, memory, and I/O, we can limit the disadvantages of sharing the same kernel between multiple containers.

The use of Docker for container management will simplify the setup of distributed systems as well as the deployment of new nodes, which can open a new era for the **platform as a service (PaaS)** mode.

Installing Docker

For Ubuntu Server 14.04 and later, Docker is part of the main Ubuntu repositories. Therefore, to install Docker, you just have to run the following command:

```
sudo apt-get install docker.io
```

For older releases, you have to update your source list before executing the installation command. This is done by performing the following steps:

1. Create a file named /etc/apt/sources.list.d/docker.list and put the following line in it:

    ```
    deb http://get.docker.io/ubuntu docker main
    ```

2. Then, download the GPG key and install the lxc-docker package by using the following command:

    ```
    sudo apt-key adv --keyserver hkp://keyserver.ubuntu.com:80 \
    --recv-keys 36A1D7869245C8950F966E92D8576A8BA88D21E9

    sudo apt-get update

    sudo apt-get install lxc-docker
    ```

> If you want to avoid using sudo with every Docker command, add the user to the Docker group by using the following command:
> ```
> sudo addgroup user docker
> ```

When the installation is finished, you have to start Docker just like any other ordinary service by using the following command:

```
service docker start
```

Using Docker

As an example, we will have a look at how to use Docker with a LAMP container. But first, let's explore some terminology that we will need later to understand different actions:

*   **DockerFile**: This is a source file that contains instructions for a configuration file

*   **Image**: This is a compilation of DockerFile that is used to build a portable image that is ready for deployment

*   **Container**: This is the execution of an image, simply a process that is used to run an image

Now, let's move on to practical stuff.

First of all, for an image, you can either prepare yours or simply download one of the prepared images built by the community. You can search for them either via the Web by visiting `https://hub.docker.com/explore/`, or via CLI by using the following command:

```
docker search lamp
```

You will get a long list of images. You have to choose your own image. For this example, we have chosen the `reinblau/lamp` image. To install this image, all that you need to do is run the following command:

```
docker pull reinblau/lamp
```

This command will download and install this image. After finishing this step, you need to run it in a container. This is done by using the `docker run` command, which can take some arguments such as the port NATing that was used in the LAMP case:

```
docker run -d -p 80:80 -p 3306:3306 reinblau/lamp
```

Here, this means that port `80` of the host machine will be mapped to port `80` of the `docker` container. The same goes for port `3306`. We can get this information from the repository page of Docker.

At this step, we can start using the LAMP server that is working in this `docker` container.

When working on a `docker` container, you will have a prompt that looks like this:

```
root@xxxxxx#
```

After you finish working, you need to save the changes on your image. To do this, you need to run the following code:

```
root@xxxxxx# exit
docker commit xxxxxx image_name
```

To list the images installed on your machine, you need to run the following code:

```
docker images
```

To list containers (the running images), you need to execute the following command:

```
docker ps -a
```

To get the job ID of your container, execute the following command:

```
docker run -d container_name
```

This job ID is useful when you need to stop a container by using the following command:

```
docker stop JOB_ID
```

When you would like to remove the job ID, use the following commands:

```
docker rm JOB-ID
docker rm container_id
```

One of the best advantages of Docker is the possibility of easily importing/exporting images.

To export a container in `tar.gz`, execute the following command:

```
docker export 2520aedc6bc5 > zimbra-after-install.tgz
```

To import a `tar.gz` file, execute the following command:

```
cat zimbra-after-install.tgz  | docker import - zimbra-after-install
```

Cloud computing for the Ubuntu Server

Cloud computing is one of the latest trends and hottest subjects in the IT world, and the Ubuntu Server is one of the leading OSes in this field, especially with its infrastructure based on OpenStack deployed by big names such as NASA, NSA, HP, AT&T, Alcatel-Lucen, and so on.

In the following section, we will explore two of the best open source Clouds that we can easily deploy on the Ubuntu Server — one for file sharing and the other for PaaS — as well as the best part concerning OpenStack deployment on Ubuntu.

The ownCloud software

The **ownCloud** software allows you to create and use a storage server and share files online. In the next section, we will see the technologies used in ownCloud software.

The technology used in ownCloud

The ownCloud software uses the WebDAV protocol to seamlessly access a server through a network drive on Linux, Windows, or Mac. There is also sync software for many platforms (Linux, Mac, Windows, Android, and so on) so that you can keep a local copy of your files and work offline. The ownCloud software not only provides a file sharing service, but also can be used to manage your calendar, contacts, bookmarks, and even music.

The project is developed in PHP. It is thus installed on many web servers. It doesn't require specific functionalities such as Java, or particular web server extensions.

In the following section, we will cover only the installation process of the ownCloud server. The installation and configuration of a client is beyond the scope of this book.

The ownCloud server installation

Since the release of version 5.0 of ownCloud, its installation is very simple. Packages for ownCloud are available for the supported versions of Ubuntu at `http://download.owncloud.org/download/repositories/stable/`.

For example, to install ownCloud for Ubuntu 15.04, run the following commands:

```
sudo sh -c "echo 'deb http://download.opensuse.org \
/repositories/isv:/ownCloud:/community/ \
xUbuntu_15.04/ /' >> /etc/apt/sources.list.d/owncloud.list
sudo apt-get update
sudo apt-get install owncloud
```

You can add the repository key to `apt`. Keep in mind that the owner of the key may distribute updates, packages, and repositories that your system will trust. To add the key, run the following code:

```
wget -nv \
https://download.owncloud.org/download/repositories/stable/ \
xUbuntu_15.04/Release.key -O Release.key


sudo apt-key add - < Release.key
```

Your server is now available at `http://<server_ip>/owncloud/`. You must create an account in the first connection. In case the server complains about unmet dependencies, restart the web server by using the `sudo service apache2 reload` command.

To enable secure connections to the Apache server (HTTPS), run the following commands:

```
sudo a2enmod ssl
sudo a2ensite default-ssl
sudo service apache2 reload
```

Now, log in to the server via `https://<server_ip>/owncloud/`. From the **Administration** menu, which is available at `https://<server_ip>/owncloud/index.php/settings/admin`, check off the **Force HTTPS** checkbox.

CozyCloud

CozyCloud is a free personal Cloud server. It focuses on applications and collaboration applications related to personal data. CozyCloud is a personal **PaaS** (**Platform as a Service**) solution that allows you to deploy personal web applications in a click. You can select the existing Cozy applications (Notes, Todos, Calendar, Contacts, Photos, and so on), adapt an existing Node.js application, or start your own web application from-scratch (documentation and tutorials related to this are available on the Internet).

Installing CozyCloud on Ubuntu Server

First of all, start by installing Python and the pip tools on your machine by using the following command:

```
apt-get install python python-pip python-dev \
software-properties-common
```

Once you have the pip tools installed on your machine, you have to install fabric and fabtools by using the following command:

```
sudo pip install fabric fabtools
```

Then, download the fabric file (a script that will run commands on your remote server), as follows:

```
wget https://raw.githubusercontent. \
com/cozy/cozy-setup/master/fabfile.py
```

Once your system is prepared, use the fabric script from your local machine to launch the Cozy installation (run it in the same directory as that of fabfile that you downloaded before). This is done by using the following command:

```
fab -H <user>@<ip_address> install
```

Once you run the preceding command, you need to be patient for a few moments. As you may know, deployments of some commands or applications can take some time depending on your network and hardware capabilities. When prompted by the installer, you have to enter your settings.

After the installation is complete, you can access https://<IP_address>:443 to create the principal Cozy account. The use of HTTPS is mandatory. In case you simply use HTTP, you will just see the nginx welcome page.

Using CozyCloud

Once the installation is complete, you can access your platform using HTTPS, as explained before. Since this is your first login, you need to register your account (provide an e-mail and a password).

 The password that you choose will also become the key that enables Cozy applications to encrypt certain information in the database.

You will then arrive at the Cozy home page that displays the installed applications. The operation is similar to that of a smartphone — you go to the marketplace (**tab +Apps**) and install the existing applications or the application that you built (if they are already on a GitHub repository).

An integral aspect of application development for CozyCloud that deserves a mention is that Cozy is a PaaS, which means that the development of an application does not depend on an SDK (as is the case with an Android or iPhone app). You can create a web application as you're used to and deploy it within Cozy or anywhere else!

 A good starting point in case you wish to document about Cozy is `https://github.com/cozy/cozy-setup/wiki`. This page contains resources related to development.

OpenStack

OpenStack is a free software that allows the construction of private and public Clouds. OpenStack is a community and a project in addition to the software that is designed to help organizations implement their own Clouds. OpenStack consists of a series of software and open source projects that are maintained by the community, which includes OpenStack Compute (named Nova), OpenStack Object Storage (named Swift), OpenStack Image Service (named Glance), and many more components that are increasing in number with every new release.

Users are mainly deploying it as an **IaaS (Infrastructure as a Service)**. This technology consists of a set of interconnected projects that control pools of processing, storage, and networking resources over a datacenter, which is managed by users through multiple utilities such as a web-based dashboard, command-line tools, or even a RESTful API.

Canonical provide a fully integrated and optimized combination of the latest release of the Ubuntu Server and the latest release of OpenStack, allowing users to get the best user experience with Ubuntu OpenStack. According to the OpenStack User Survey that was conducted in November 2014:

> *64% of production OpenStack clouds are run on Ubuntu.*

Canonical provides a set of useful tools. When associated with OpenStack, they give it more dimensions. In this section, we will start by discovering these tools. Then, we will move on to see how to install OpenStack in an Ubuntu Server.

OpenStack tools

As mentioned previously, Ubuntu is the most popular operating system for OpenStack in the world. Ubuntu offers a set of innovative tools and programs that help users build their enterprise-scale Cloud in the easiest and fastest way.

Juju

Juju, which also means magic, is the service orchestration management tool that was mainly developed by Canonical for Cloud computing. Juju concentrates on services. It provides a new concept of software deployment in an easy and quick manner with possibilities of integration and scalability on a large number of Cloud infrastructures. One of the primary components of Juju is called Charms, which can be written in any programming language that can be executed from the command line.

MAAS

The concept of **Metal as a Service** (**MAAS**) was created by Canonical to provide a system that can simplify the task of setting up a physical hardware on which you can deploy complex scalable services in the same manner as that of Ubuntu's OpenStack Cloud infrastructure does.

MAAS takes care of preparing the new node, installing the Ubuntu image, configuring it, and making it functional. Besides, it checks hardware-specific tasks, such as burn-in tests, firmware, and the RAID upgrade.

The MAAS and Juju combination will breathe new life into old hardware by recycling it for use in other parts of your infrastructure.

Landscape

The official management tool for Cloud computing under the Ubuntu Server is Landscape. It is one of the most powerful tools of the Ubuntu OpenStack combination. It is a rich web-based GUI that allows users to easily build its Cloud in minutes, monitor it in real time, and manage it in the most efficient way.

LXD

Also known as the Linux container hypervisor, LXD is the next-generation hypervisor provided by Canonical. It combines the density of containers with the manageability of virtual machines. LXD simplifies deployment and the running of VMs in a connected and secure environment with high-scalability possibilities and the ability of interoperability.

Snappy

Snappy is a Cloud-based operating system provided by Canonical and based on the Ubuntu Server. It was developed to be used with **Internet of Things (IoT)** devices. The difference between the Snappy Ubuntu core and the standard Ubuntu system is that applications are provided through a simpler, faster mechanism and most importantly, it provides a stronger security guarantee for apps, making it ideal for Docker and other Cloud deployment frameworks.

The OpenStack setup

Mastering OpenStack, from its setup, configuration, and administration, to troubleshooting and maintenance, are subjects that need to be explained in books with hundreds of pages. In this section, we don't have much space to elaborate on all of this. So, I will try to make you get a taste of it. We will discover the main lines steps of setting up an OpenStack Cloud on an Ubuntu Server in two ways—the manual installation and the DevStack-based installation.

Installing OpenStack using DevStack

DevStack is a script that can be used to quickly create an OpenStack development environment or demonstrate OpenStack services and provide examples of using them from a CLI. It changed from a simple demonstration tool to a useful, quick sanity check for the OpenStack installation.

The mission of DevStack is to provide and maintain tools used for the installation of the central OpenStack services from the source (the `git` repository master or specific branches) suitable for development and operational testing. It also demonstrates and documents examples of configuring and running services as well as using command-line clients.

The following are the steps needed to install OpenStack using DevStack:

1. Install the selected OS. In our case, it is Ubuntu Server 15.04.

2. Download DevStack by using the following command:

   ```
   git clone https://git.openstack.org/openstack-dev/devstack
   ```

3. The `devstack` repository contains a script that installs OpenStack and templates for configuration files.

4. Configure your environment. You can refer to http://docs.openstack.org/developer/devstack/configuration.html for more details.

5. Start the installation by using the following command:

```
cd devstack; ./stack.sh
```

It takes a few minutes to run the preceding command. We recommend that you read the preceding script while it is being installed.

 You can find a lot of guides at http://docs.openstack.org/developer/devstack/.

The manual installation

The manual installation is actually the most suitable for you if you want to deploy a real Cloud and not just to test the power of OpenStack. We can install the Cloud on only one machine, but it is recommended by Canonical that you should use at least seven machines, each with two hard disks, and two of them must have two **network interfaces (NICs)**.

 If you want to just set up OpenStack on a single Ubuntu Server based on the 14.04 LTS or 15.04 releases, a good tutorial is available at https://fosskb.wordpress.com/2015/04/18/installing-openstack-kilo-on-ubuntu-15-04-single-machine-setup/.

However, in case you want to get a real Cloud according to the Canonical recommendations, the following is a summary of the steps that are required if you wish to get your own Cloud OpenStack running based on the Ubuntu servers:

1. First of all, you have to install the Ubuntu Server on one of the machines that have two network interfaces. Then, you need to set up a private network with all the machines plugged in, with the network divided into the following three logical ranges:

    ○ The dynamic range maps an IP address to every NIC connected to the network

    ○ The static range maps an IP address to every machine connected to the network

    ○ The floating IP range maps an IP address to every instance that you'll have in your Cloud

2. Secondly, you need to add the needed repositories to your source list and update your package list by using the following commands:

    ```
    sudo add-apt-repository ppa:juju/stable

    sudo add-apt-repository ppa:maas-maintainers/stable

    sudo add-apt-repository ppa:cloud-installer/stable

    sudo apt-get update
    ```

3. Next, if you want to set up MAAS, you need to run the following command:

    ```
    sudo apt-get install maas
    ```

4. Now, perform the following step-by-step instructions:

    ○   Access the MAAS UI at `http://<maas_ip_address>/MAAS/` and follow the instructions provided there to create a profile of an administrator. Then, log in with those credentials.

    ○   Import disk images for Ubuntu.

    ○   Add the SSH key to your user profile by visiting `http://<maas_ip_address>/MAAS/account/prefs/`.

    ○   Copy the MAAS key (you will need this later).

    ○   Fill in the other details, such as the gateway and DNS, in the networks that were automatically created for each NIC.

    Next, you need to configure the MAAS cluster, as follows:

    ○   Click on the **Clusters** tab and select **Cluster master**.

    ○   You will see a list of network interfaces on the machine. Click on the edit symbol for the interface that is connected to the private network where all the nodes are visible.

    ○   Set this interface to manage DHCP and DNS.

    ○   Set the router IP to the default gateway for this private network.

    ○   Fill in the details for the dynamic and static ranges; remember that you should leave gaps for the floating IPs.

    ○   Save the changes.

    Now, you need to enlist and commission the machines, as follows:

    ○   Ensure that all the machines are set to the **Preboot Execution Environment (PXE)** boot. If possible, disable all the other boot options, including local disk in the BIOS.

- ° Enlist the machines by powering them on. This can usually be done by some sort of a virtual console. They will all appear in the node list in MAAS, and they can be powered down again.

- ° Edit each machine in the node's list and fill in the power type and power parameters (that is, the username and password) so that MAAS can turn them on and off as needed.

- ° Select all the machines and, by using the **Bulk action** dropdown, commission them.

- ° Wait until all the machines are commissioned (that is, in the `Ready` state).

5. At this point, you need to set up `Landscape` and launch the OpenStack `Autopilot` by using the following commands:

```
sudo apt-get install openstack
sudo openstack-install
```

6. Choose the **Landscape OpenStack Autopilot** option.

7. Fill in the MAAS credentials using the MAAS key that you saved when you set up MAAS.

8. Open the link to access the Landscape UI.

9. Resolve the remaining issues on the checklist. Finally, click on the **Configure** button.

10. Go to the given URL to get to the landing page of the Landscape UI.

11. The landing page contains a checklist at the bottom that shows the status of all your resources. Verify that all of them are green to confirm the sanity status of your infrastructure.

12. Click on **Configure** and enter an optional name for your region and Cloud.

13. Select the following components (this is an initial list; more options will be added in the later versions as they pass the tests in the OpenStack Interoperability Lab):

    - ° The hypervisor component (KVM)

    - ° The networking component (Open vSwitch)

    - ° The storage components:

      Object (Ceph, Swift)

      Block (Ceph, iSCSI)

14. Select the hardware on which you need to deploy the Cloud and click on **Save selection**.

15. Click on **Install** to build your Cloud.

16. Finally, start using your Cloud!

Summary

In this chapter, we focused on one of the most interesting features of the Ubuntu Server, namely virtualization and Cloud computing. At this point, you can define and easily use a good set of programs related to this subject on the Ubuntu server.

In the next chapter, we will discover some useful tips that an Ubuntu system administrator needs to make their life easier.

6
Tips and Tricks for Ubuntu Server

This is the last chapter of this essential book. In this chapter, we will take a look at a collection of the best tips and tricks that every Ubuntu Server administrator needs to simplify their life when administering their servers based on Ubuntu.

This chapter is divided into the following three sections:

- General tips – a set of generic tips related to the CLI, configuration, and scripting
- Troubleshooting tips – helpful tips for troubleshooting tasks
- Useful tools and utilities – a set of tricky programs with high added value to the system administrator

General tips

In this section, we will explore some useful tips and tricks for Ubuntu Server. These are general tips related to the **command-line interface** (**CLI**), package management, and the customization of configurations.

Ubuntu Server CLI tips and tricks

The following are some useful CLI commands:

1. Get the reason behind installing a package, that is, check the reverse dependencies of the given package, by using the following command:

    ```
    apt-cache rdepends --installed [package_name]
    apt-cache rdepends --installed mysql-server
    ```

2. List all the users along with their respective last login time by executing the following command:

```
lastlog
```

3. To change the server time zone, you need to run the following code:

```
sudo dpkg-reconfigure tzdata
```

Furthermore, to check whether the `timezone` has changed or not, you need to run the following command:

```
less /etc/timezone
```

Also, don't forget to restart `cron` so that it can pick up the `timezone` change, as follows:

```
sudo service cron restart
```

4. If you need to manually synchronize your server time, use the following command:

```
sudo ntpdate ntp.ubuntu.com
```

5. In case you want to install a time synchronization service, execute the following command:

```
sudo apt-get install ntp
```

6. To update the hardware clock, run the following command:

```
hwclock --set --date '`date`'
```

7. To list all the mounted and unmounted partitions on your server, use the following command:

```
sudo fdisk -l | less
```

8. If you just want to list the mounted partitions and the free space on each of these partitions, use the following command:

```
df -h
```

9. View the size of a particular file or folder by using the following code (this is very important when viewing the size of folders):

```
du -h myfile
du -sh myfolder
```

10. As a file grows, you can view the appended data with the help of the following code (this is useful for monitoring and troubleshooting):

```
tail -f filename
less +F filename
```

11. Get the system environment variables by using the following command:

```
printenv
```

12. To change the server hostname, execute the following code:

```
sudo sh -c "echo new_host_name > /etc/hostname"
sudo /etc/init.d/hostname restart
```

13. To view information about the Linux distribution, you need to execute the following command:

```
lsb_release -a
```

14. To find out the OS installation date, run the following command:

```
ls -ld /var/log/installer
```

How to prevent server daemons from starting during installation

In some circumstances, we don't want a server or daemon to start as part of a post-installation script when installing updates with apt-get or dpkg. To reach this goal, you need to create a file named policy-rc.d under the /usr/sbin/ directory and put the following content in it:

```
#!/bin/sh

exit 101
```

Then, give it the *755* rights by using the following command:

```
chmod 755 /usr/sbin/policy-rc.d
```

When you finish, don't forget to remove this file by using the following command:

```
rm -f /usr/sbin/policy-rc.d
```

How to move or copy a directory

The copy (cp) command only works for files. To copy a directory, you need to use the -r recursive flag, as follows:

```
cp -r input_directry destination_directory
```

The move (mv) command works the same way. You need to use the -r recursive flag to move a directory, as follows:

```
mv -r input_directry destination_directory
```

System resource limits

The default behavior in Ubuntu Server is to not impose resource limits on user processes. This means that users are free to use all of the available memory on the machine or launch processes in an endless loop, thus rendering the system unusable in seconds. The best solution to this is limiting some user resources by editing the `/etc/security/limits.conf` file with the help of the following command:

```
sudoedit /etc/security/limits.conf
```

The content of the file is well explained. Besides, there is a good `man` page for the configuration of this file:

```
man limits.conf
```

For disk quotation, you need to install the quota package, as discussed in an earlier chapter of this book.

Running a command over and over

Sometimes we need to run the same command again and again to either monitor the progress of an operation of copying a file, or troubleshoot the status of a server. Though you can run the same command over and over, a better method is to use the `watch` command. The `watch` program takes a command as an argument and then runs that command every two seconds, showing its output on the screen. So for instance, if we want to monitor the size of `ubuntu.iso`, we will type `watch "ls -l ubuntu.iso"`. The `watch` command accepts a few arguments, such as the `-n` argument, so that you can adjust how many seconds it will wait before it runs the program again.

Troubleshooting tips

In this section, you will find advanced tips related to the troubleshooting of tasks. They are a must for most Ubuntu Server administrators.

Customizing log rotation on Ubuntu Server

The best starting point for troubleshooting a problem is reading the related service log. Logs are not saved infinitely; they are kept on the system and they follow a specific policy. After a span of time, the oldest logs are dropped. Thus, we keep only some of the latest log files. This is called **log rotation**; it is done on Ubuntu Server on two levels. The generic policy is configured in the `/etc/logrotate.conf` file, and a specific policy is configured for some services in a specific file under the `/etc/logrotate.d/` directory.

This specific file, named `/etc/logrotate.d/*` is not commented, but the `/etc/logrotate.conf` generic file is very expressive and well commented and has a syntax that is the same as that of the specific file. There is also good documentation about this on the `man` page, which can be viewed by executing the following command:

`man logrotate`

Some of the parameters that exist on these files by default are as follows:

- The **periodicity of log rotation**, rotation can be set in such a way that the log rotation is performed daily, weekly, monthly, and so on
- The **lifetime of each log file**, that is, the period for which a log file is kept on the system before being deleted, is expressed in weeks and associated with the `rotate` parameter
- An **option to compress log files** is available with an aim to save space by using the `compress` parameter

Some of the other parameters that can be added manually are as follows:

- The `delaycompress` parameter postpones the compression of the previous log file to the next rotation cycle, thus allowing users to easily view last week's log without having to uncompressing it
- The `dateex` directive changes the default backlog file name from the default behavior (numerically naming the files: `logname.0`, `logname.1`, `logname.2`, and so on) to include the *YYYYMMDD* date pattern instead of 0, 1, 2, and so on.

The main system log files

System log files are the pillar of every troubleshooting task. Going through them carefully often allows system administrators to discover in advance when something is wrong with the system and resolve most problems before they escalate.

Usually, logs files are stored under the `/var/log` directory; and for a server that has been running for a while, there are a lot of older versions of log files in that directory, and most of them are compressed with `gzip`.

The following are some log files of note:

- The general system log: `/var/log/syslog`
- The system authentication logs: `/var/log/auth.log`
- The system e-mail logs: `/var/log/mail.log`

- The general log messages: `/var/log/messages`
- The kernel ring buffer messages, usually when the system boots up: `/var/log/dmesg`

Checking opened files

Sometimes when troubleshooting we need to check for a specific file (check which process is running and currently opening it), or for a specific filesystem (which files are open on it and for which use). This information is provided by the `lsof` command. In the `lsof` output, you will see a list of all the processes along with the open files on that filesystem, their process IDs, the user, and the size of the resources allocated to them.

Getting information from /proc

A good starting point for the troubleshooting of Ubuntu Server is getting information about the state of processes, hardware devices, kernel subsystems, and other attributes of Linux. This can be done via the `/proc` files.

Getting information from files in the `/proc` directory is simply done by using the `cat` command. Under `/proc`, you will see a separate directory for every running process (each has its PID as a name) containing information about that process. You will also find the `/proc` files that contain general data for all kinds of other measurements, such as the computer's CPU, software versions, disk partitions, memory usage, and so on.

Here's a list of examples that illustrate the information that you can get from your Ubuntu system's `/proc` directory:

- To show the options that were used in the boot prompt, run `cat /proc/cmdline`
- To show information related to the server processor, run `cat /proc/cpuinfo`
- To show the existing character and block devices, run `cat /proc/devices`
- To display disks, partitions, and statistics, run `cat /proc/diskstats`
- To list the filesystem types in the current kernel, run `cat /proc/filesystems`
- To show the physical memory addresses, run `cat /proc/iomem`
- To show the virtual memory addresses, run `cat /proc/ioports`

- To show the 1-, 5-, and 15-minute load averages, and the running processes/ the total and the highest **Process Identification Number** (**PID**), run `cat /proc/loadavg`

- To show the available RAM and swap memory, run `cat /proc/meminfo`

- To show the loaded modules, memory size, instances loaded, dependencies' load state, and kernel memory, run `cat /proc/modules`

- To show the mounted local/remote filesystem information, run `cat /proc/mounts`

- To show the mounted local disk partitions, run `cat /proc/partitions`

- To show the RAID status (when using RAID software), run `cat /proc/mdstat`

- To show the kernel stats since the system was booted, run `cat /proc/stat`

- To display information about swap space, run `cat /proc/swaps`

- To display the kernel version and the related compiler, run `cat /proc/version`

Recovering the root password under Ubuntu Server

Sometimes, server administrators can't remember the root password. On Ubuntu Server, recovering the root password can be done by booting the system under a specific mode called a **single user mode**, which is also called **runlevel 1** or the **Recovery Mode**.

So, the first step is to enter this mode by using the GRUB menu. Normally, on Ubuntu Server, you will find this entry automatically (it has the `Recovery Mode` tag between the parentheses after the GRUB entry name). If this is not the case, use GRUB to manually edit the proposed menu entry at the time of booting by adding the word "single" at the end of the line of the boot entry that you want.

The kernel should boot as usual, but you will get a root prompt (`sh#`) instead of the ordinary prompt (`sh$`).

At this point, we have gained root access to the filesystem. We can finally change the password. Now you have root access, when changing the password you will not be asked for your old password. So, on running the following command, you will be asked for your new password and its confirmation directly:

```
# passwd
```

Finally, you can now reboot your machine and gain root access again.

By default, the filesystem is read-only in the recovery mode. It needs to be remounted as read/write mode in order to change the root password or do any other task that needs writing on the disk. To mount it with read/write access mode, enter the following command:

```
mount -o remount,rw /
```

Note the spaces: you'll get an error in case you ignore the spacesor add extra ones.

If you have /home, /boot, /tmp, or any other mount point on a separate partition, you can mount them with the help of the following command:

```
mount --all
```

However, you must do this just after the first remount step so that /etc/mtab is writable.

Useful tools and utilities

In this section, we will have a look at some tools and utilities that help Ubuntu Server administrators to manage their systems in the best way needs so that systems usability is boosted to its maximum.

NetHogs, a network monitoring tool

NetHogs is a network monitoring tool that helps you identify the program that consumes your bandwidth. It is a kind of top command, but it's for network. This tool is very useful when you are troubleshooting network issues such as **what is hogging the Internet connection?**.

To launch nethogs, you need to do it with root privileges by using sudo command, because it relies on libpcap to sniff the network, like most network monitoring tools.

The installation of nethogs is simple, you just need to run the following command:

```
sudo apt-get install nethogs
```

After the installation, you can start using it via the following command:

```
sudo nethogs network_interface_card (by default without using the NIC
it will use eth0), for example: sudo nethogs eth1
```

Once the program is running, you can use the *M* key to switch between the following two modes:

- The real-time usage
- The total usage (different modes exist based on the size unit, such as KB, MB, and so on)

vnStat, a network monitoring tool

While `nethogs`, the tool that we saw in the last section, allows you to monitor your network bandwidth usage in real time by collecting statistics at a given date/time, it cannot give you a hand if you wish to monitor bandwidth usage over an hour/day/week/month. This tricky function is provided by another network monitoring tool named `vnStat`. The `vnstat` daemon is a suite of programs that monitor network bandwidth usage.

To install `vnStat` on Ubuntu Server, you can use `apt-get`, as follows:

```
sudo apt-get install vnstat
```

The configuration of `vnStat` is done by editing the `/etc/vnstat.conf` file; just don't forget to restart `itwith`, as follows:

```
sudo /etc/init.d/vnstat restart
```

To start the `vnStat` daemon, execute the `vnstatd` command

Before using this tool, you need to wait for some time for data to be collected, and then run the `vnstat` command.

There are a lot of helpful options that come with this tool. You can discover them by using the `man` page. The following are the most useful ones:

- `vnstat -h`: This is used to see the summary of the hourly usage
- `vnstat -d`: This is used to see the summary of the daily usage
- `vnstat -w`: This is used to see the summary of the weekly usage
- `vnstat -m`: This is used to see the summary of the monthly usage
- `vnstat -t`: This shows the all-time top 10 traffic days.
- `vnstat -tr 10`: This shows the usage over x seconds (default value is 5)
- `vnstat -l`: This shows the live bandwidth usage

`vnStat` is a useful little tool if you want to get a good overview of how much bandwidth you use on a hourly/daily/weekly/monthly basis, and it requires almost no resources to do so.

Tailing multiple files using multitail

In many cases, a system administrator needs to tail multiple files at the same time. There is a sweet Linux tool named `multitail` that provides this function. The `multitail` tool will let you tail multiple files at the same time within the same shell. Besides this main function, `multitail` allows you to run multiple commands and tail their outputs, which simplifies the lives of system administrations, especially for some advanced troubleshooting tasks.

To install this tool, you just need to run the following command:

```
sudo apt-get install multitail
```

There are a lot of ways to use this command. You can refer to the `man` page, where there are different examples that explain how to better customize output.

The program cockpit – a remote manager for Ubuntu servers

The `cockpit` command is an interactive server administrator interface. It is easy to use and very lightweight. It allows an Ubuntu Server administrator to perform a lot of tasks, such as storage administration, journal and log inspection, and services management (starting and stopping) in a user-friendly interface.

To install `cockpit` on Ubuntu Server, you have to run the following commands:

```
sudo add-apt-repository ppa:jpsutton/cockpit
sudo apt-get update
sudo apt-get install cockpit
```

To start the `cockpit` service, use the following command:

```
sudo systemctl start cockpit
```

If you want to start the `cockpit` service automatically when you reboot your server, use the following command:

```
sudo systemctl enable cockpit.socket
```

Finally, to access the `cockpit` GUI, use the following URL:

```
https://<server_ip>:9090
```

Webmin: the famous system administration tool

Webmin is one of the most famous Unix administration tools. It is a web-based interface that provides a huge set of functionalities to easily manage server resources, including: the setting up of user accounts; the administration of services such as Apache, FTP, DNS, and so on; the management of sharing files; and a lot of other functions. All in all, it is a user-friendly interface.

Installing webmin needs, before anything else, you to have a fully functional and running LAMP server. We discussed how to get this done in *Chapter 3, Deploying Servers on Ubuntu*, of this book.

After that, you need to install webmin from the APT repository. First of all, you need to add the webmin official repository to your server source list file. This is done by editing the /etc/apt/sources.list file using the sudo vi /etc/apt/sources.list command. Then add the following lines to sources.list file:

```
deb http://download.webmin.com/download/repository sarge contrib
deb http://webmin.mirror.somersettechsolutions.co.uk/repository sarge contrib
```

After doing this, you need to download the **GNU Privacy Guard** (**GPG**) key and add it to the APT keys by using the following commands:

```
wget http://www.webmin.com/jcameron-key.asc
sudo apt-key add jcameron-key.asc
```

Next, update the source list by using the following command:

```
sudo apt-get update
```

Finally, install webmin by using the following command:

```
sudo apt-get install webmin
```

To access webmin, you need to go to https://<server_ip>:10000.

Using the uvtool program and extending the use of Cloud images

The uvtool program is provided by Canonical for the Ubuntu administrators who want to use the already-prepared Cloud images outside the Cloud infrastructure to create a virtual machine without the need of a complete installation of Cloud servers. This greatly facilitates the task of generating VMs using Cloud images.

Installing uvtool is simple, just use the following command:

```
sudo apt-get -y install uvtool
```

> The details as regard to using uvtool to find and synchronize Cloud images and create and manage VMs and the other functionalities provided by this powerful tool, that can be seen in the rich official documentation that is available at https://help.ubuntu.com/lts/serverguide/cloud-images-and-uvtool.html.

Summary

In the last chapter of this essential book, we had a look at some of the best tips and tricks that Ubuntu Server administrators need to manage their Ubuntu servers in an easy, efficient, and powerful way. At this point, you have the necessary knowledge and skills to fly high with one of the best OSes in the ICT world.

Index

A

administration tasks
  configuring, with sudo 82
advanced installation, Ubuntu
  about 12
  LVM, using 14-16
  RAID, using 13, 14
advanced security configuration
  about 87
  firewalls, configuring 89-92
  SSH security enhancement 87-89
Amavisd-new 65-67
Apache
  stopping 59
apache2ctl
  about 59
  commands 59
Apache management 58
Apache tools
  about 58
  apache2ctl 59
AppArmor tool
  configuring 83-87
approaches, towards virtualization
  full virtualization 105
  paravirtualization 105
apt (Advanced Packaging Tool) 31
aptitude tool 31, 32
apt tools
  about 32
  apt-get tool 32
Areca Backup 97

automated installation, Ubuntu
  about 16
  additional resources 20
  PXE process 16

B

BackInTime 97
backup
  database backups 94-96
  drive imaging 93
  performing 92
  principles 93
Backup-Manager 98
BackupPC 97
backup tools
  about 96-99
  well-known tools 97
Bacula 97
bare-metal hypervisor 103
basic security settings
  about 75
  user quota, applying to user accounts 81, 82
  users, managing 75
brute force attack 78

C

ClamAV 67
Clonezilla 98
Cloud computing, for Ubuntu server
  about 119
  CozyCloud 121
  OpenStack 122
  ownCloud software 119

command-line interface (CLI) 129
complain mode 86
container 102
CozyCloud
  about 121
  installing, on Ubuntu server 121
  using 122

D

database server
  MySQL server 69
  Postgre server 70
  setting up 69
Déjà Dup 97
DHCP (Dynamic Host Control Protocol) 70
DHCP server
  configuring 71
  installing 71
  setting up 70
  Ubuntu DHCP conventions 71
DNS server
  about 49
  BIND, configuring 51
  BIND installation 50
  DNS redundancy 53
  DNS testing 54
  setting up 49
  Ubuntu BIND conventions 51
  zone file configuration 51, 52
Docker
  about 116
  installing 117
  using 117-119
  working 116
DockerFile 117
DomainKeys Identified Mail (DKIM) 67
dpkg tool 29, 30
Duplicity 98
dynamic DHCP 71

E

e-mail server
  facilities 68
  filters and security 65

end of file (EOF) signal 24
enforce mode 86

F

file server
  FTP server 72
  installing 72
  Samba server 72

G

GNU Privacy Guard (GPG) key 139
GRand Unified Bootloader (GRUB) 113
greylisting 67

H

hosted hypervisor 103
HostKey directive 49
hypervisor
  about 102
  type 1 hypervisor 103
  type 2 hypervisor 103, 104

I

IaaS (Infrastructure as a Service) 122
Image 117
IMAP 60
Internet of Things (IoT) 124
isolator 102-104

J

Juju 123

K

KVM (Kernel-based Virtual Machine)
  about 101-105
  installing 109
  networking, configuring 107, 108
  prerequisites 106
  virtual machines, managing 110, 111

L

LAMP installation
  performing 55, 56
  Ubuntu LAMP conventions 56-58
LAMP (Linux Apache MySQL PHP) 54
Landscape 123
log rotation 132
LuckyBackup 97
LVM (Logical Volume Manager)
  using 14-16
LXC (Linux Containers) 2, 116

M

mail server
  deploying 60
  MDA server 64, 65
  MTA server 61
main repository 26
manual installation, Ubuntu
  about 3
  installation from CD 4-11
  upgrading 11, 12
Master Boot Recorder (MBR) 11
MDA (Mail Delivery Agent) 60
MDA server 64, 65
Metal as a Service (MAAS) 123
MTA (Mail Transfer Agent)
  about 60
  Postfix, installing 61-63
  Postfix, managing 63, 64
MTA server 61
multitail
  using 138
multiverse repository 26
MySQL server 69

N

native hypervisor 103
NAT (Network Address Translation) 107
NetHogs 136
network configuration, Ubuntu server
  about 36
  configuration files 37

  network utilities 38, 39
network interfaces (NICs) 125

O

OpenDKIM 67
OpenSSH server
  about 47
  configuration 48, 49
  deploying 47
  installing 48
OpenStack
  about 122
  installing, DevStack used 124
  Juju 123
  Landscape 123
  LXD 124
  MAAS 123
  manual installation 125-127
  setting up 124
  Snappy 124
  tools 123
OpenXenManager 115
operating-system-level virtualization 102
Oracle VirtualBox 103
ownCloud software
  about 119
  installing 120
  technology 119

P

PaaS (Platform as a Service) 121
package management 25
package management utilities
  about 28
  aptitude tool 31, 32
  apt tools 32, 33
  dpkg tool 29, 30
  tasksel tool 35
packages repositories
  about 26-28
  main 26
  multiverse 26
  restricted 26
  universe 26

paravirtualization approach 105
Partclone 98
permission settings
  about 78
  file ownership 78
  permissions, configuring 79, 80
Personal Package Archives (PPA) 26
phpMyAdmin 55
POP 60
Postfix
  about 61
  installing 61-63
  managing 63, 64
  postconf command 64
  postqueue command 64
  postsuper command 64
Postgre server 70
Postgrey 67
Preboot Execution Environment (PXE) 126
prerequisites, Ubuntu server installation
  about 1
  additional resources 3
  latest Ubuntu release 1, 2
  system requirements 2
Primary Domain Controller (PDC) 72
Process Identification Number (PID) 135
program cockpit 138
PV (physical volume) 14
PXE (Preboot Execution Environment)
  about 16
  installation procedure 16-19

R

RAID (Redundant Array of Inexpensive
    Disks)
  about 13
  using 13, 14
restricted repository 26
Rsync 98

S

Samba server 72, 73
SBackup 97

Sender Policy Framework (SPF) 67
Sendmail Mail Filter (Milter) 67
SFTP (SSH File Transfer Protocol) 72
single user mode 135
SMTP 60
Snappy 124
spam 65
Spamassassin 67
static DHCP 71
system administration tasks, Ubuntu server
  performing 40
  processes, managing 43, 44
  processes, scheduling for run 44, 45
  resources, monitoring 40-43
system calls 23

T

tasksel tool
  about 35
  used, for adding software collections 35
tips and tricks
  command, executing 132
  directory, copying 131
  directory, moving 131
  for Ubuntu Server CLI 129-131
  server daemons, avoiding at
      installation 131
  system resource, limiting 132
tools and utilities
  multitail 138
  NetHogs 136
  program cockpit 138
  uvtool program 140
  vnStat 137
  Webmin 139
troubleshooting tips
  information, obtaining from / proc
      files 134, 135
  log rotation, customizing 132, 133
  opened files, checking 134
  root password, recovering 135, 136
  system log files 133, 134

U

Ubuntu server
  administering, command line used 21-24
  network configuration 36
  package management 25
  system administration tasks, performing 40
Ubuntu Server CLI
  tips and tricks 129-131
Ubuntu server installation
  about 1
  advanced installation 12
  automated installation 16
  manual installation 3
  prerequisites 1
Unison 98
universe repository 26
Unsolicited Bulk Email (UBE) 65
user account administration
  -e date option 76
  -G groups 77
  -m option 76
  about 76
  passwd command 76
  useradd command 76
  userdel command 76
  usermod command 76
user management
  about 75
  password administration 77
  permission settings 78
  user account administration 76
user quota
  about 81
  applying, to user accounts 81
utilities, for e-mail server
  Amavisd-new 65
  ClamAV 67
  OpenDKIM 67
  Postgrey 67
  Spamassassin 67
uvtool program
  URL 140
  used, for extending Cloud images
    usage 140

V

VEs 102
VG (volume group) 14
Virt-manager 115
virtualization
  about 101, 102
  approaches 105
  benefits 102
  Docker 116
  hypervisor 102
  isolator 104
  KVM (Kernel-based Virtual Machine) 105
  techniques 102
  XenServer 111
virtualization engine 102
virtual machines (VMs) 102
vnStat
  about 137
  options 137

W

Webmin 139
web server
  Apache management 58
  LAMP installation 55, 56
  turning on 54

X

XCP Project Kronos 115
Xen Cloud Platform 115
XenServer
  about 103-112
  domain 0 OS 111
  domain U machines 112
  installing 113
  networking 114
  prerequisites 112, 113
  virtual machines, managing 115
xen-tools 115

Thank you for buying
Ubuntu Server Essentials

About Packt Publishing

Packt, pronounced 'packed', published its first book, *Mastering phpMyAdmin for Effective MySQL Management*, in April 2004, and subsequently continued to specialize in publishing highly focused books on specific technologies and solutions.

Our books and publications share the experiences of your fellow IT professionals in adapting and customizing today's systems, applications, and frameworks. Our solution-based books give you the knowledge and power to customize the software and technologies you're using to get the job done. Packt books are more specific and less general than the IT books you have seen in the past. Our unique business model allows us to bring you more focused information, giving you more of what you need to know, and less of what you don't.

Packt is a modern yet unique publishing company that focuses on producing quality, cutting-edge books for communities of developers, administrators, and newbies alike. For more information, please visit our website at www.packtpub.com.

About Packt Open Source

In 2010, Packt launched two new brands, Packt Open Source and Packt Enterprise, in order to continue its focus on specialization. This book is part of the Packt Open Source brand, home to books published on software built around open source licenses, and offering information to anybody from advanced developers to budding web designers. The Open Source brand also runs Packt's Open Source Royalty Scheme, by which Packt gives a royalty to each open source project about whose software a book is sold.

Writing for Packt

We welcome all inquiries from people who are interested in authoring. Book proposals should be sent to author@packtpub.com. If your book idea is still at an early stage and you would like to discuss it first before writing a formal book proposal, then please contact us; one of our commissioning editors will get in touch with you.

We're not just looking for published authors; if you have strong technical skills but no writing experience, our experienced editors can help you develop a writing career, or simply get some additional reward for your expertise.

Microsoft Exchange Server 2013 High Availability

ISBN: 978-1-78217-150-8   Paperback: 266 pages

Design a highly available Exchange 2013 messaging environment using real-world examples

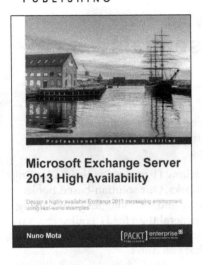

Microsoft Exchange Server 2013 High Availability

Design a highly available Exchange 2013 messaging environment using real-world examples

Nuno Mota

1. Use the easy-to-follow guidelines and tips to achieve the highest availability.

2. Covers all the aspects that need to be considered before, during and after implementation of high availability.

3. Packed with clear diagrams and scenarios that simplify the application of high availability concepts such as site resilience.

SQL Server Analysis Services 2012 Cube Development Cookbook

ISBN: 978-1-84968-980-9   Paperback: 340 pages

More than 100 recipes to develop Business Intelligence solutions using Analysis Services

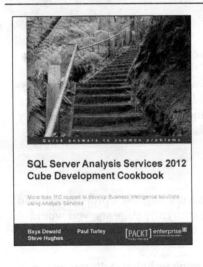

SQL Server Analysis Services 2012 Cube Development Cookbook

More than 100 recipes to develop Business Intelligence solutions using Analysis Services

Baya Dewald   Paul Turley
Steve Hughes

1. Develop Business Intelligence solutions using a multi-dimensional model as well as a tabular model.

2. Explore cube maintenance with partitions and design effective aggregations, as well as analyzing options for scaling analytics solutions.

Please check **www.PacktPub.com** for information on our titles

Building Web and Mobile ArcGIS Server Applications with JavaScript

ISBN: 978-1-84969-796-5   Paperback: 274 pages

Master the ArcGIS API for JavaScript, and build exciting, custom web and mobile GIS applications with the ArcGIS Server

1. Develop ArcGIS Server applications with JavaScript, both for traditional web browsers as well as the mobile platform.

2. Acquire in-demand GIS skills sought by many employers.

3. Step-by-step instructions, examples, and hands-on practice designed to help you learn the key features and design considerations for building custom ArcGIS Server applications.

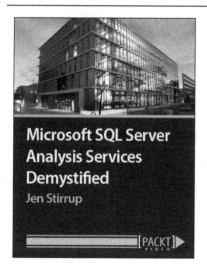

Microsoft SQL Server Analysis Services Demystified [Video]

ISBN: 978-1-84968-930-4   Duration: 02:17 hours

Design, implement, and deliver a successful business intelligence project with SQL Server Analysis 2012 Services

1. Learn how to make the correct design choice between multidimensional and tabular models according to your project requirements.

2. Learn the key implementation features of Analysis Services cubes and how to visualize data.

3. An essential two hour course to get you familiar and productive with the basics of data analysis.

Please check **www.PacktPub.com** for information on our titles